THE NEW
PASTA
COOKBOOK

JOANNE GLYNN

MURDOCH BOOKS®
Sydney • London • Vancouver • New York

CONTENTS

The Pasta Story

Pasta's popularity has always been its adaptability. It can come in many different forms, with taste differences and visual variety; it is cheap, quickly and easily prepared; it can be a meal in itself or eaten with other foods such as meat and vegetables. Pasta has a high nutritional value and is an easily digested source of energy.

Pasta is a dough made from flour, water and/or eggs. The flour used for commercial pasta is made from milled durum wheat in the form of semolina, a coarsely ground meal. Dough made from durum wheat semolina absorbs less water and will dry easily; holds together well during kneading, drying and cooking; withstands pressure well; has a better texture and 'bite' and reheats successfully.

Eggs are sometimes added to commercial dried pasta to give extra body and flavour. Homemade pasta nearly always uses eggs which give the dough flavour and make it manageable and easy to roll.

Buying Pasta

Bought pasta falls into three main categories:

Packaged dry pasta (*pasta secche*) which is available from every supermarket shelf. It is worth checking the labels to establish that durum wheat semolina has been used (*pasta di semolina di grano duro* on Italian imports) and for the use or exclusion of egg (*all' uovo* means with eggs). Cooking time for this pasta is 10 minutes or more as it needs to re-hydrate as well as cook.

Fresh pasta (*pasta fresca*) is available from specialty pasta shops and delicatessens and in the refrigerator in supermarkets. It is often displayed in bulk and you can purchase as little or as much as you need. This pasta is quite pliable and takes a very short time to cook (1½ to 3 minutes).

Dried, pre-packed 'fresh pasta' falls between the other two categories and is available from supermarkets, delicatessens and food shops. Cooking time is 3 to 5 minutes.

Hints on Cooking

The success of a pasta dish depends on the correct cooking of the pasta you have chosen to use.

Firstly, the proportion of water to pasta is important. Too little, and the pasta will be crowded and unable to cook evenly. It will go gluey as the relatively small amount of water becomes starch laden. There can never be too much water. Use a minimum of 4 litres water to every 500 grams pasta; use more if cooking dried pasta, as it absorbs more water.

Use a very large pot. Bring the water to a rolling boil. Just before putting in the pasta add a dash of oil (to help prevent sticking) and a large pinch of salt (a knob of rock salt or unrefined sea salt for preference) which helps bring out the flavour. If using fresh pasta, shake it gently to loosen the strands before adding it to the water.

Once the pasta is in, stir to move it off the bottom of the pot. When the water comes back to the boil start timing, maintaining a slow rolling boil. Don't stir too often now as this tends to release excess starch.

The pasta is done when it is *al dente*: tender, but with some resistance to the bite. You should feel the texture and form in the mouth, not mushy dough. Moreover, if the pasta is overcooked it cannot physically support the rest of the ingredients and won't allow for an even distribution of the sauce. Taste the pasta just before the time is up. Note: As fresh pasta takes only a couple of minutes to cook, its timing is more critical.

Don't be over zealous in draining, as it is desirable to leave a little of the cooking water to help with lubrication. Only rinse if the pasta is intended to be used as a cold dish.

Next, stir through a little oil or melted butter. This helps with the final saucing and stops the pasta sticking together. Lastly, always have the waiting bowls and serving dishes warmed.

HOMEMADE PASTA

Plain flour is usually used when making egg pasta. It gives a fine textured, light dough which is well suited to filled pastas such as ravioli, as it gives the pasta good elasticity.

The addition of durum wheat semolina gives a better colour, more flavour and a resilient texture, as well as providing the nutritional benefits of hard wheat flours. The proportion of semolina to plain flour is a matter of choice but a maximum of two-thirds semolina and one-third plain flour is recommended. In making pasta with other flours such as wholemeal or buckwheat, this point should be kept in mind as different meals and grains have differing absorption levels and 'short' qualities.

Eggs used should be the freshest available, as their freshness not only influences the flavour and colour of the pasta, but also the elastic quality of the dough.

The standard proportion of eggs to flour is 1 medium egg to every ¾ cup (90 g) flour, and a pinch of salt is generally added. It is sometimes necessary to use a little water, but this will depend on the particular flours used and the humidity at the time. Eggless pasta is made the same way as egg pasta except that the eggs are replaced in volume by water.

The only equipment you need is a board and a long rolling pin. However, a food processor takes the labour out of mixing, and a hand-cranked pasta machine simplifies and takes the guesswork out of rolling and cutting.

For a basic dough, you need 1½ cups (200 g) plain flour, 2 eggs, a large pinch salt and some water. This amount is enough to serve two main courses or three entrées.

MIXING BY HAND Use a pastry board or a large bowl. Put flour in a mound with a well in the centre. Add eggs and salt, and start blending with a fork or fingers, incorporating more and more of the flour into the eggs and working from the inside outward. When flour and eggs are combined, start to knead the dough on the board incorporating extra flour or adding water as necessary.

It will take about 5 minutes to get a smooth, firm dough. If durum wheat semolina is used, allow a good 7 to 10 minutes of kneading. It takes this time for the hard semolina to absorb moisture and develop its strong, pliable characteristics.

Only experience can tell you when the dough is ready. It should not be sticky or wet to the touch. If you can knead it well without adding flour, it is probably ready.

When finished, cover the dough with a tea-towel or upturned bowl to prevent a crust forming, and rest it for at least 15 minutes.

MIXING IN A PROCESSOR Fit the metal blade. Add dry ingredients to the bowl. With the motor running, add eggs through the feed tube. After 5 seconds a ball should form. If the dough is still sticky, add flour until a ball forms, or the machine slows down or stops. Alternatively, a few drops of water may be necessary to take the dough from the meal

stage. Take the dough out and knead it until elastic, 2 to 3 minutes. Rest dough as above.

ROLLING AND CUTTING BY HAND Divide the dough into manageable balls and keep them covered until needed. Working ball by ball, press out the centre with your hand. Using a long rolling pin, roll each evenly and smoothly with a little flour on the board.

Lift and turn the dough often, and don't be in a hurry; you want an even, thinly rolled sheet of pasta. The pasta will swell a little with cooking, so roll it thinner than the desired cooked thickness. For filled pastas the dough should be next to paper thin.

When you're happy with the proportions, cover each sheet with a layer of plastic, and then the lot with a dampened tea-towel to prevent drying out.

If the dough is to be cut into strips like tagliatelle, let it rest to dry slightly; this prevents the ribbons from sticking together. Then cut the sheets into rectangles approximately 25 cm long and roll these up, jelly roll style, along their length. Using a sharp knife and with smooth strokes, cut uniform slices which unroll to become, for example, tagliatelle (0.5 cm wide), pappardelle (2 cm wide) or whatever pasta type you decide to make.

ROLLING AND CUTTING WITH PASTA MACHINE Starting with the rollers on the widest setting, roll a flattened ball of dough through two or three times. Fold the dough in thirds and roll again. Repeat this process four or five times or until the dough is a smooth and elastic sheet of even proportions. Now pass the dough through the rollers with them set at decreasing widths apart, until the desired thickness is reached. Avoid adding flour. If dough becomes sticky, a light dusting should help it through.

If, before cutting, the dough seems too wet, let it sit uncovered for 15 minutes or so. It should be dry enough so that the cut lengths won't stick together but will still pass through the cutters without cracking. Crank the sheets of dough through the required cutting rollers.

Try a combination of semolina and flour

Making your own pasta is easy and fun

Spread the cut lengths on a dry tea towel, or hang them over the backs of chairs or a broom handle until ready to cook. Pasta made entirely with plain flour doesn't dry well; it tends to crack as the moisture evaporates.

MAKING FILLED PASTA The thinly rolled sheets should be kept under a damp tea-towel or plastic sheets and used quickly.

Have the filling ready before the pasta so that you're ready to go as soon as the dough is made.

There are three main ways of making filled shapes:

i) Using a Mould: these are trays pressed with the grooves and ridges of different shaped and sized raviolis, which usually come with their own little rolling pin to seal and cut the dough around the filling. They are useful when a uniformly sized and cut pasta is desired.

ii) Sheeted Filling: this is a successful way of making many ravioli quickly. Cut two sheets of dough, one slightly bigger than the other. On the smaller sheet place spoonfuls of filling at even intervals, then brush along the intended cutting lines with beaten egg. Position the larger sheet of pasta over the top neatly and run over the cutting lines with your finger to make sure that both sheets of pasta are touching together. Now cut the shapes out with a floured pastry wheel. The best one to use is a cutter/crimper which cuts and seals at the same time, but a zig-zag wheel is also effective.

iii) Folded by Hand: this method gives a well-sealed ravioli as each one is pressed together by hand.

Roll out pasta smoothly and evenly with a rolling pin

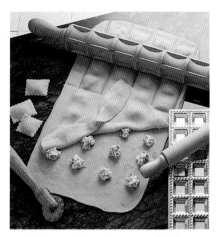

Special pasta making equipment makes the task easy

Working one sheet of pasta at a time, cut out the shapes required (round for a half moon ravioli; squares for triangles; rectangles for squares) and brush the borders with beaten egg.

Place a spoonful of filling to one side of the centreline of each. Fold the dough over the filling to match corresponding edges, press between the fingers and then seal the cut edge with a pastry cutter.

Place finished stuffed pasta on a tray or plate dusted with semolina or rice flour and store in the refrigerator before cooking.

Fettuccine

Lasagnette

Spirelli (Fusilli)

Herb taglierini

Black pepper fettuccine

Paglia e fieno

Lasagne

Spinach spaghetti

F resh Pasta – for taste, texture, temptation.

Today an integral part of a truly balanced diet.

Cooks in minutes for that minimum effort maximum result meal.

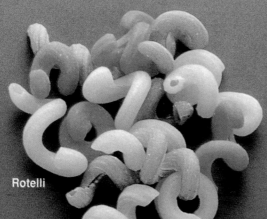

Rotelli

Conchiglie

Fettuccine —tomato, spinach and egg

Egg spaghetti

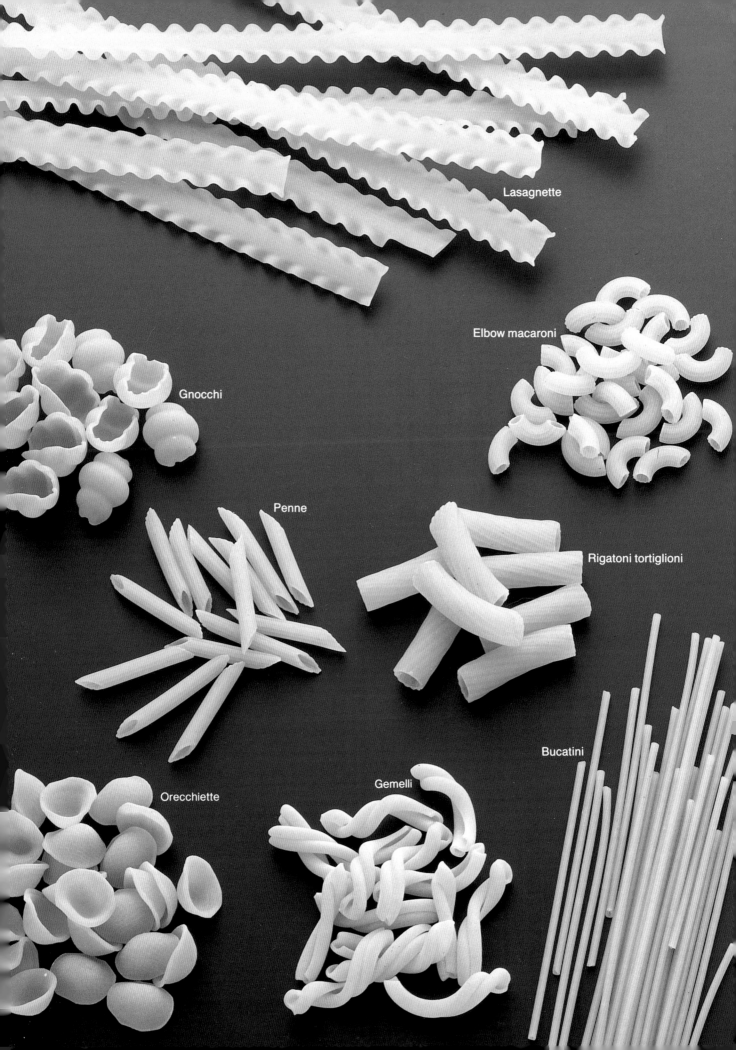

Lasagnette

Elbow macaroni

Gnocchi

Penne

Rigatoni tortiglioni

Bucatini

Orecchiette

Gemelli

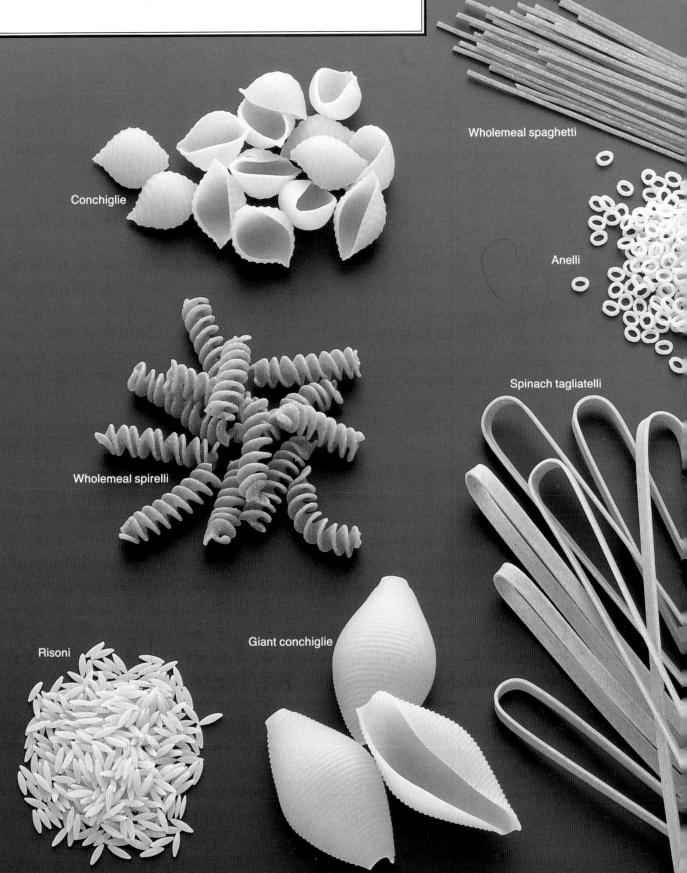

Dried Pasta available in more shapes and sizes than there are days of the year – rings for soups, rolled sheets for baking dishes, large shells for stuffing and all those long lengths for tempting sauces.

Wholemeal spaghetti

Conchiglie

Anelli

Spinach tagliatelli

Wholemeal spirelli

Risoni

Giant conchiglie

Some dishes rely on a small, subtle coating of the pasta, while others require the pasta to be secondary to a hearty sauce. As a guideline, allow 100 grams of dried pasta per adult for a main meal and 60 to 70 grams for an entrée or small helping. If cooking fresh and homemade pasta, 150 grams is a good main course serve, 80 to 100 grams for entrée. And what you don't finish can always be eaten the following day!

BEGINNINGS

What better way to start a meal than with a bowl of pasta, delicately sauced or tossed with other flavourful ingredients? Pasta takes so many forms and guises that there is always something appropriate to serve. Many of these recipes make excellent light meals, served with a salad.

PRAWN AND BASIL SOUP

2 tablespoons olive oil

20 g butter

2 cloves garlic

1 small red onion, thinly sliced

2 stalks celery, cut in 2 to 3 cm strips

3 small carrots, thinly sliced

1 tablespoon finely chopped fresh parsley

1½ tablespoons finely chopped fresh basil

salt and freshly ground black pepper

pinch cayenne pepper

500 g medium uncooked prawns (shrimps), peeled and deveined

½ cup (125 ml) medium dry sherry

4 cups (1 litre) chicken stock

70 g small conchiglie

3 tablespoons cream

fresh basil, extra, to garnish

1 In a large saucepan heat oil and butter. Add garlic cloves and onion and sauté gently for 2 to 3 minutes.

2 Add celery and carrots and fry until vegetables are golden; do not brown. Toss in parsley and basil and season to taste. Stir briefly, add prawns, toss through, then remove garlic cloves.

3 Pour in sherry, increase heat and cook for 2 to 3 minutes. Add chicken stock, bring back to the boil then simmer for 5 minutes.

4 Add conchiglie and simmer until pasta is *al dente*.

5 Stir in cream, adjust seasonings to taste and serve garnished with basil leaves.

SERVES 4

BROCCOLI SOUP

2 tablespoons olive oil

1 large onion, thinly sliced

50 g diced prosciutto or unsmoked ham

1 clove garlic, crushed

5 cups (1.25 litres) chicken stock

50 g stellini or other pastina

250 g broccoli, tops cut into small florets and the tender stems julienned

salt and freshly ground black pepper

freshly grated Parmesan cheese

1 Heat oil in a large pan and gently sauté onion, prosciutto and garlic for 4 to 5 minutes.

2 Pour in stock, bring to the boil and simmer for 10 minutes with the lid three-quarters on.

3 Add stellini and broccoli and cook until pasta is *al dente* and broccoli crisp but tender. Season to taste. Serve in warm bowls, handing round the Parmesan.

SERVES 4

Prawn and Basil Soup (top) and Broccoli Soup

PUMPKIN AND LEEK SOUP

700 g pumpkin pieces, skin left on

60 g butter

2 leeks, white part only, thinly sliced

1 large Spanish onion, chopped

350 g potatoes, peeled and diced

2 cups (500 ml) milk

2 cups (500 ml) chicken stock

70 g risoni or orzo

salt and white pepper

pinch cayenne pepper

1 cup (250 ml) cream

1 tablespoon finely chopped fresh mint

1 Preheat oven to 190°C (375°F).

2 Place pumpkin pieces skin side up and close together in a large baking dish. Pour over ½ cup (125 ml) water and bake for about 1 hour.

3 Melt half the butter and gently fry leeks until softened. Remove from the pan and fry onion and potatoes in remaining butter until golden. Add milk and boil gently for 20 minutes. Don't worry if the milk reduces; just make sure that there is enough liquid to prevent sticking to the pan.

4 When pumpkin is tender and golden, remove from oven, cool, then remove skin and any excessively browned surfaces.

5 In the meantime put chicken stock on to boil, add risoni and cook until barely done. Remove pasta with a slotted spoon and set aside with leeks. Reserve stock.

6 Now blend pumpkin and potato mixture in a food processor or force through a fine sieve. Season with salt, pepper and cayenne to taste.

6 Transfer to a clean saucepan and blend in the hot stock. Add cream, bring to the boil, and then stir in leeks and pasta. If the soup is too thick, thin it with extra stock or water. Adjust seasoning and stir in mint.

SERVES 4 TO 6

Pumpkin and Leek Soup

SPINACH FUSILLI AND ZUCCHINI SALAD

If fresh bocconcini aren't available, don't substitute ordinary mozzarella but choose a fresh, white cheese such as feta or stracchino.

150 g spinach fusilli

120 g small zucchini (courgettes), sliced

4 anchovy fillets, soaked in milk for 45 minutes

250 g celery, sliced, plus some coarsely torn tender leaves

180 g cherry tomatoes or small tomatoes cut into wedges

150 g bocconcini, cut into small pieces

1 tablespoon fresh basil leaves, roughly torn

DRESSING

⅓ cup (80 ml) white wine vinegar

¼ cup (60 ml) olive oil

salt and freshly ground black pepper

1 Cook fusilli in boiling salted water until just *al dente*. Drain, rinse under cold water and drain again. Transfer to a salad bowl and stir through a little vegetable oil.

2 Sprinkle zucchini with a little salt and let draw in a strainer for 30 minutes. Rinse, drain, and add to the bowl.

3 Pat dry the anchovy fillets, reserve two for decoration and cut the others into small pieces. Add to the salad bowl with celery and leaves, tomatoes, bocconcini and basil.

4 TO PREPARE DRESSING: Combine vinegar, oil, salt and pepper in a jar. Dress the salad, tossing lightly to coat. Garnish with reserved anchovies, cover with plastic wrap and refrigerate for at least 1½ hours before serving.

SERVES 4

≈ **PUMPKIN AND LEEK SOUP**

Baking the pumpkin gives it a special mellow flavour, but if you're pushed for time it can be skinned and boiled with the potatoes.

≈ **BOCCONCINI**

These are little balls of mozzarella with a life of 4 to 5 days. They are eaten for their own sake and usually not used as a melting cheese. Don't substitute matured mozzarella for bocconcini.

≈ **SALAD TRICOLORE**

This is just as good when made with other cold poultry; the crunch of the sesame seeds and crisp spinach leaves are a good foil for tender poultry meat.

SALAD TRICOLORE

250 g fresh tomato rotelli or 180 g dried tomato shapes

1 teaspoon peanut oil

200 g sliced cooked chicken

¼ cup (40 g) sesame seeds, toasted

1 large bunch English spinach or silverbeet, rinsed and dried, torn into pieces

1 bunch spring onions, sliced thinly, including some green

DRESSING

¼ cup (60 ml) peanut oil

¼ cup (60 ml) olive oil

¼ cup (60 ml) soy sauce

¼ cup (60 ml) rice wine vinegar

1 to 2 tablespoons caster sugar

salt and freshly ground black pepper

1 Cook pasta in boiling salted water until *al dente*. Drain, rinse under cold water and drain again. Put in a large salad bowl and stir through peanut oil. Cool.

2 Add chicken and sesame seeds.

3 TO PREPARE DRESSING: In a jar combine all ingredients and shake well.

4 Pour dressing over salad. Cover and chill for at least 2 hours.

5 To serve, toss spring onions and spinach through the salad.

SERVES 4 TO 6

≈ **RICOTTA GNOCCHETTI**

These gnocchetti can be served as a tasty side dish with a stew or casserole.

RICOTTA GNOCCHETTI

350 g dry ricotta cheese

1¼ cups (150 g) plain flour

2 tablespoons fine white breadcrumbs

150 g Parmesan cheese, grated

2 eggs plus 2 egg yolks, beaten together

salt, white pepper and nutmeg

80 g butter

1 In a bowl combine ricotta, flour, breadcrumbs, half the Parmesan and eggs. Add a pinch each of the seasonings and

blend to form a smooth dough which is dry to the touch. It may be necessary to add a little more flour or a few drops of milk to get the right balance: the moistness of the ricotta will determine this.

2 Knead the dough well, then rest, loosely covered, for 15 minutes. Using your hands, roll the dough into two or three long ropes, 1.5 cm in diameter. Again rest for 15 minutes before slicing diagonally into 2 cm lengths.

3 Cook gnocchi in boiling unsalted water for 3 minutes. In the meantime melt butter and cook over a low heat until golden brown. Drain gnocchi and pile on a warm serving plate. Pour over butter and sprinkle with remaining Parmesan before serving.

SERVES 4

TUNA GNOCCHI SALAD

250 g broccoli, broken into florets

250 g cauliflower, broken into florets

250 g dried gnocchi shells pasta shapes, not dumplings

1 bunch spring onions, sliced, including some of the green

4 small tomatoes, cut into wedges

1 clove garlic, thinly sliced

3 tablespoons finely chopped fresh Italian parsley

½ cup (125 ml) extra virgin olive oil

juice 1 small lemon

½ teaspoon sea salt

freshly ground black pepper

440 g canned tuna in olive oil, drained

1 Bring a large saucepan of water to the boil, add a pinch of salt and pop in the broccoli and cauliflower. Cook for 2 to 3 minutes; they should be still crisp and not soft. Remove from the pan with a slotted spoon and rinse under cold water. Shake them dry and transfer to a large serving bowl.

2 To the same boiling water add pasta and

cook for 15 minutes, or until *al dente*. Rinse under cold water and shake dry. Transfer to the salad bowl.

3 Add spring onions, tomatoes, garlic, parsley, olive oil, lemon juice, salt and pepper to the bowl and mix together lightly.

4 Coarsely flake tuna into bite-sized pieces and toss through the salad. Serve at room temperature.

SERVES 4 AS A LIGHT MEAL

BEAN AND PASTA SALAD

250 g pennette or other small hollow shape pasta

600 g cooked cannellini beans (or any small white beans)

1 small red onion, thinly sliced

1 thin stalk celery, sliced

2 small tomatoes, cut in wedges

60 g small black olives

fresh oregano leaves, to garnish

DRESSING

½ cup (125 ml) extra virgin olive oil

1½ teaspoons Dijon-style mustard

juice 1 lemon

1 tablespoon finely chopped fresh oregano or parsley

salt and freshly ground black pepper

1 clove garlic, crushed

1 Cook pennette in boiling salted water until *al dente*. Drain, rinse under cold water and drain again. Transfer to a large serving bowl, stir through a little of the oil to prevent sticking together, and cool.

2 Add beans, onion, celery, tomatoes and olives.

3 TO PREPARE DRESSING: Combine all ingredients in a jar and shake well.

4 Pour dressing over salad. Toss thoroughly and taste for salt and pepper. Cover and chill. When ready to serve, toss again lightly and garnish with oregano leaves.

SERVES 4

SAFFRON RISONI SALAD

350 g risoni

½ cup (125 ml) olive oil

1 g pure saffron powder

1 cup (125 g) pine nuts

½ cup (60 g) currants

2 cloves garlic, crushed

juice 1 lemon

¼ teaspoon ground cumin

1 teaspoon ground turmeric

½ teaspoon sugar

salt and freshly ground black pepper

1 small green capsicum (pepper), thinly sliced in 1 to 2 cm lengths

2 tablespoons finely chopped fresh parsley

2 tablespoons finely chopped fresh mint

2 tablespoons finely chopped fresh coriander

coriander leaves, for garnish

1 Cook risoni in boiling salted water for a minute or two less than recommended. Drain, rinse in cold water and drain again. Stir through a little olive oil to prevent sticking.

2 Heat oil in a small pan and add saffron, pine nuts and currants. Cook gently until nuts are toasted and saffron gives off its unique aroma. Remove from heat and add garlic, lemon juice, cumin, turmeric, sugar, salt and pepper to taste. Stand for at least 5 minutes.

3 Add capsicum, herbs and pine nut mixture to the pasta. Toss before serving, garnished with coriander leaves.

SERVES 4 TO 6 AS A SIDE DISH

≈ **SAFFRON RISONI SALAD**

This delicious spicy 'rice' salad is slightly sweet and so is a perfect accompaniment for grilled or barbecued meals.

*When using pasta in
a salad, it is important
to rinse the cooked pasta
with cold water and
drain it well. Toss
a little oil through
the pasta to stop it
sticking together.*

PASTRAMI, MUSHROOM AND CUCUMBER SALAD

*As pastrami is from a lean cut of beef, this dish is low in
kilojoules and high in protein and vitamins.*

200 g lasagnette, broken into quarters

250 g pastrami, cut in strips

1 stalk celery, sliced

2 small tomatoes, cut in wedges

**1 Lebanese cucumber about 30 cm long,
thinly sliced**

80 g button mushrooms, thinly sliced

**¼ teaspoon finely chopped fresh coriander,
for garnish**

DRESSING

¼ cup (60 ml) olive oil

2 tablespoons red wine vinegar

½ teaspoon Dijon-style mustard

salt and freshly ground black pepper

1 clove garlic, crushed

¼ teaspoon hot chilli oil

1 Cook lasagnette in boiling salted water
until *al dente*; drain and rinse under cold
water, then drain again before transferring to
a salad bowl.

2 To the salad bowl add pastrami, celery,
tomato wedges, cucumber and mushrooms.

3 TO PREPARE DRESSING: Combine
ingredients in a jar and shake well to blend.

4 Toss the dressing through the salad and
refrigerate, covered, for several hours.

5 Adjust seasoning and sprinkle with
coriander before serving.

SERVES 4

TUNA, GREEN BEAN AND ONION SALAD

*This salad is equally good served warm or refrigerated
overnight and served the next day.*

**200 g stringless green beans, trimmed and
cut in 3 cm lengths.**

**300 g short pasta shapes
(fusilli or penne rigate)**

½ cup (125 ml) olive oil

**250 g fresh tuna fillet, sliced in
3 to 4 cm pieces**

1 red onion, thinly sliced

1 teaspoon balsamic vinegar

salt and freshly ground black pepper

1 In a large pan of boiling water cook beans
for 1 to 2 minutes until tender-crisp.
Remove with a slotted spoon and rinse
under cold water. Drain and transfer to a
serving bowl.

2 Add pinch salt to boiling water then
cook pasta until *al dente*. Drain, rinse under
cold water then drain again before adding
to beans.

3 In a frying pan heat half the oil. Add tuna
and onion. Sauté until tuna is just cooked
through. Add vinegar, turn up heat and
quickly cook until dressing has reduced and
lightly coats tuna. Transfer tuna and onion
to a bowl, leaving behind any bits on the
bottom of the pan.

4 Toss beans, pasta, tuna and onion together
lightly and mix with remaining oil, and salt
and pepper to taste. Cool to room
temperature before serving.

SERVES 4

*Tuna, Green Bean and Onion Salad (above) and
Pastrami, Mushroom and Cucumber Salad (below)*

Pastina is the generic term for all tiny pasta shapes usually served in soups.

STUFFED CAPSICUMS AND TOMATOES

The capsicums and tomatoes can be eaten hot or cold, and can be served as a first course, a light meal or part of a buffet. They are a good accompaniment to lamb, veal or chicken.

3 large tomatoes, stalk ends sliced off

3 green capsicums (peppers), stalk ends and seeds removed.

3 to 4 tablespoons chicken or vegetable stock

FILLING

2 tablespoons olive oil

1 large onion, chopped

2 cloves garlic, crushed

¼ teaspoon cayenne pepper

salt and freshly ground black pepper

1 tablespoon currants

1 tablespoon pine nuts

1 tablespoon chopped fresh coriander

1 teaspoon chopped fresh parsley

1½ cups cooked risoni or other pastina

100 g matured Cheddar or Emmenthaler cheese, grated

1 Preheat oven to 180°C (350°F).

2 TO PREPARE FILLING: Heat oil and gently sauté onion and garlic until soft. Add cayenne, salt and pepper to taste, currants, pine nuts, coriander and parsley. Sauté until nuts are lightly brown. Transfer to a bowl and combine with pasta and cheese.

3 Scoop pulp from tomatoes, chop finely and add to filling. Mix well.

4 Divide filling between capsicum and tomato cases, stuffing lightly. Put capsicums into a shallow ovenproof dish, pour a tablespoon of stock over each and bake for 30 minutes.

5 Add tomatoes to the dish and bake for a further 20 minutes, or until tender.

SERVES 6

LUMACHE WITH ARTICHOKES

3 tablespoons olive oil

1 large onion, roughly chopped

2 cloves garlic, crushed

3 teaspoons dried basil

1½ tablespoons chopped fresh parsley

pinch chilli powder

1 teaspoon dried oregano

1.6 kg canned Italian peeled tomatoes, drained, (reserve juice)

¼ teaspoon salt

350 g lumache, pipe rigate or other multi-surfaced shape

440 g canned artichoke hearts, drained, (reserve juice)

2 tablespoons grated pecorino cheese

1 Heat oil in a large pot and sauté onion, garlic, basil, parsley, chilli and oregano for 5 minutes.

2 Roughly chop tomatoes and add them to the pot with the salt. Simmer, uncovered, for about 45 minutes, or until reduced and very thick. Add reserved tomato and artichoke juices, stir through and simmer a further 15 minutes.

3 Cook lumache in boiling salted water until *al dente*.

4 Cut each artichoke heart into six and toss them through the sauce along with pecorino.

5 Drain cooked pasta and add to sauce. Stir well, transfer to warm dishes and serve, handing around extra cheese.

SERVES 4

PORCINI MUSHROOMS

The unforgettable taste of fresh porcini or boletus mushrooms cooked in butter is closely matched by using a combination of the dried variety and fresh plump button mushrooms. Choose large ones with lots of white flesh to duplicate the texture and appearance of fresh porcini; flat field mushrooms have too much dark gill section and aren't recommended.

LINGUINE WITH MUSHROOMS

10 g dried porcini or boletus mushrooms

30 g butter

1 small onion, finely chopped

400 g very large button mushrooms, sliced

**1 tablespoon chopped fresh sage
(don't substitute dried)**

1 tablespoon finely chopped fresh parsley

salt and freshly ground black pepper

400 g fresh linguine or 300 g dried

**4 tablespoons freshly grated
Parmesan cheese**

1 Soak porcini mushrooms in ¾ cup
(180 ml) warm water for 45 to 60 minutes.
Drain off liquid and then filter it through
muslin or a paper coffee filter to remove grit.
Finely slice the rehydrated mushrooms.

2 Melt half the butter in a frying pan and
gently sauté onion until soft and golden.
Add porcini and filtered liquid and cook
until evaporated. Add remaining butter,
button mushrooms and herbs. Season well
and gently simmer, covered, for 15 to
20 minutes.

3 Meanwhile, cook pasta in boiling salted
water until *al dente*; drain, and toss with the
sauce, and Parmesan.

SERVES 4

SPINACH PASTA FRITTATA

50 g Parmesan cheese, grated

5 eggs

½ cup (125 ml) milk

½ cup (125 ml) cream

1 tablespoon olive oil

1 tablespoon plain flour

salt and pepper

250 g cooked spinach spaghetti or fettuccine

2 teaspoons chopped fresh herbs (parsley, oregano, chives)

1 tablespoon pine nuts

LIFESTYLE IMPORTS PTY LTD

1 Preheat oven to 180°C (350°F).

2 In a bowl blend thoroughly Parmesan,
eggs, milk, cream, oil and flour, and season
well with salt and pepper. Stir through pasta
and herbs.

3 Grease a 20 cm round ovenproof pie dish,
and line it with 2 crossed strips of foil;
grease these. Pour in pasta custard, and
sprinkle pine nuts on top. Bake for about
35 minutes, until set and golden.

4 Remove from oven and cool slightly
before lifting out, using the foil strips as
handles. Serve warm or cold.

SERVES 4 TO 6 AS A LIGHT MEAL WITH SALAD

*Linguine with
Mushrooms*

≈ FRITTATAS

*Frittatas are a great way
of using pre-cooked pasta.
To the basic egg and
pasta mixture can be
added pieces of ham,
salami, mushrooms or
cheese. Even leftover
sauced pasta can be used,
provided that the sauce
isn't too runny.*

Pasta Flan

PENNE PARCELS

250 g penne

1 tablespoon olive oil

2 onions, thinly sliced

4 red capsicums (peppers), cut into thin strips

5 small tomatoes, cut into thin wedges

3 cm sprig fresh rosemary

salt and freshly ground black pepper

2 small zucchini (courgettes), julienned

½ cup (125 ml) chicken stock

1 Preheat oven to 190°C (375°F).

2 Cook pasta in boiling salted water and drain a minute or two before it's done.

3 Heat oil in a large frying pan and sauté onions and capsicums until onions are soft and golden, 10 to 12 minutes; do not brown.

4 Add tomatoes and rosemary, and season to taste. Cook over a low heat, partly covered, for 10 minutes, stirring often.

5 Add zucchini and stock and cook for a further 3 to 4 minutes or until there is about ¼ cup (60 ml) liquid left. Remove rosemary and check seasoning. Stir through penne.

6 Cut four large sheets of aluminium foil (about 30 cm square) and divide the pasta mixture between them. Fold over the foil of each parcel and wrap it up tightly so that no steam can escape. Place the bundles in a shallow baking dish and bake for 15 minutes. Serve immediately, being careful of escaping steam when opening the parcels.

SERVES 4

≈ PASTA PARCELS

Baking pasta and its sauce in a parcel expands the flavours and entraps moisture, keeping the dish succulent. Many pasta-based dishes can be completed this way. Slightly undercook the pasta initially, to leave enough liquid in the sauce for the food to steam. Seal the parcels well.

PASTA FLAN

BASE

175 g vermicelli

1 tablespoon oil

2 eggs, lightly beaten

large pinch ground nutmeg

2 tablespoons finely grated fresh Parmesan cheese

salt and freshly ground black pepper

FILLING

½ cup (125 ml) olive oil

1 clove garlic, crushed

800 g canned Italian peeled tomatoes

grated rind ½ large orange

1 tablespoon finely chopped fresh mint

large pinch sugar

100 g fontina cheese or Bel Paese, cut into small cubes

1 Preheat oven to 190°C (375°F).

2 TO PREPARE BASE: Cook vermicelli in boiling salted water until *al dente*. Drain and stir through 1 tablespoon olive oil.

3 In a large bowl combine eggs, nutmeg and Parmesan and season with salt and pepper. Add vermicelli and stir well to coat pasta evenly with egg mixture.

4 Grease a 22 cm round pie dish and press the pasta evenly over the bottom and up the sides to form a shallow rim.

5 Cover the rim loosely with a strip of foil and bake for 10 minutes, or until set. Don't remove the foil. Leave oven setting.

6 TO PREPARE FILLING: Heat oil in a frying pan and gently sauté garlic for 1 minute. Drain tomatoes, reserving juice, and break them up with a wooden spoon before adding to the pan. Cook over a low heat for 5 minutes, stirring occasionally. Add salt and pepper to taste, 4 tablespoons of reserved tomato juice and orange rind. Simmer until tomatoes are pulpy and thick, stirring from time to time. The mixture should be quite dry with no excess liquid.

7 Remove from heat and stir in mint and sugar, then leave to cool slightly. Stir the cheese into the tomato mixture and then spoon it into the pasta base.

8 Bake until set, about 30 minutes. Cool slightly before serving.

SERVES 6

PAPPARDELLE WITH SALAMI

2 teaspoons olive oil

1 teaspoon butter

½ small onion, finely chopped

1 clove garlic, crushed

125 g salami, thinly sliced and cut into strips

½ cup (125 ml) dry white wine

400 g canned Italian peeled tomatoes, drained

1 red capsicum (pepper), chopped

1 tablespoon sultanas

1 tablespoon pine nuts

salt and freshly ground black pepper

pinch each ground nutmeg and sugar

½ cup (125 ml) cream

400 g pappardelle

½ teaspoon chopped fresh mint

1 tablespoon freshly grated Parmesan cheese

1 Melt oil and butter in a large saucepan and gently sauté onion and garlic for 5 minutes. Add salami and then wine, cooking over a high heat to evaporate.

2 Squeeze seeds and juice from tomatoes, leaving a very dry pulp. Add this to the pan along with capsicum, sultanas and pine nuts. Season to taste and stir in nutmeg and sugar. Reduce heat and cook, covered, for 15 to 20 minutes. Add cream and stir through.

3 Meanwhile, put pappardelle on to cook in boiling salted water. When *al dente*, drain and add to the saucepan with mint. Toss to coat, stir in Parmesan and transfer to a warm serving dish. Serve with extra Parmesan handed round.

SERVES 4

≈ **PASTA PIE BASES**

Pasta pie bases are an interesting way of using pre-cooked ribbon pastas. Smaller nests for individual servings are also attractive: these look good with chopped parsley or perhaps poppy seeds stirred through the pasta mixture before baking.

≈ **PAPPARDELLE WITH SALAMI**

A sauce with a sweet intense flavour, this can be made lighter by omitting the salami and keeping the proportions of the other ingredients the same.

ROTELLI WITH TOMATOES AND GREEN OLIVES

9 or 10 ripe tomatoes, peeled, seeded and cut into chunks

⅔ cup (100 g) stoned green olives, sliced

2 cloves garlic, crushed

3 tablespoons finely chopped fresh parsley or basil, or a mixture

salt and freshly ground black pepper

½ cup (125 ml) extra virgin olive oil

2 to 3 drops balsamic vinegar

350 g fresh rotelli or 275 g dried

1 Combine tomatoes, olives, garlic, herbs, salt and pepper in a large serving bowl. Add olive oil and vinegar and toss to coat well. Cover and stand at room temperature for at least 2 hours to allow the flavours to develop.

2 Cook rotelli in boiling salted water until *al dente*; drain and toss through the sauce immediately before serving.

SERVES 4

RIGATONI WITH RICOTTA

280 g rigatoni or other large hollow tubes

vegetable oil

80 g unsalted butter, melted

freshly grated Parmesan cheese

fresh sage or mint leaves

FILLING

280 g dry ricotta cheese

80 g Parmesan cheese, freshly grated

salt and nutmeg

1 Cook rigatoni in boiling salted water until *al dente*; drain, and stir through a little vegetable oil. Cool slightly.

2 Preheat oven to 190°C (375°F).

3 TO PREPARE FILLING: In a bowl combine ricotta and Parmesan, and add salt and nutmeg to taste. Using an icing bag with a 1 to 2 cm nozzle, stuff each tube well with the ricotta filling.

4 Place tubes in a greased, shallow ovenproof dish and pour over the butter to cover them well. Sprinkle with some Parmesan and toss in a couple of sage leaves. Bake for 15 minutes.

5 Transfer to a warm serving plate, replace the sage leaves with fresh ones and serve.

SERVES 4

SPINACH FETTUCCINE WITH ANCHOVIES

400 g fresh spinach fettuccine or 280 g dried

ANCHOVY SAUCE

40 g butter

2 tablespoons olive oil

1 small onion, finely chopped

4 to 6 anchovy fillets, finely chopped

80 g button mushrooms, sliced

freshly ground black pepper

EGG SAUCE

2 egg yolks

1 cup (250 ml) cream

2 tablespoons grated Parmesan cheese

freshly ground black pepper

1 teaspoon chives cut into 1 cm lengths

1 Cook fettuccine in boiling salted water until *al dente*.

2 TO PREPARE ANCHOVY SAUCE: Heat butter and oil in a saucepan and gently sauté onion for 5 minutes. Add anchovies and sauté. Add mushrooms and toss to coat. Stir in 2 tablespoons of pasta water. Season with pepper.

3 TO PREPARE EGG SAUCE: Beat together egg yolks, cream and Parmesan.

4 Drain fettuccine and stir it through mushrooms. Add egg sauce and chives. Toss until fettuccine is well coated and the sauce is heated through and slightly thickened. Serve with extra Parmesan and black pepper.

SERVES 4

Penne with Eggplant and Pecorino

PENNE WITH EGGPLANT AND PECORINO

This dish is rich and strong. You can add other vegetables such as zucchini (courgettes) and olives. For a lighter version using less oil, quickly toss diced eggplant (aubergine) in oil then put under the grill, turning a couple of times, until browned.

700 g young, firm eggplant (aubergine), cut in 2 cm cubes

1 cup (250 ml) olive oil

2 cloves garlic, crushed

½ medium-sized green capsicum (pepper), thinly sliced

400 g canned Italian peeled tomatoes, strained and pulped

salt and freshly ground black pepper

500 g fresh penne or 380 g dried

1 tablespoon chopped fresh basil or 1½ tablespoons fresh parsley

40 g pecorino cheese, grated

1 Place eggplant in a large colander and sprinkle with salt. Leave for at least 30 minutes for the bitter juices to be drawn out by the salt. Squeeze off excess liquid before frying.

2 In a large frying pan, heat some of the oil and fry eggplant in batches, adding more oil as needed. As each lot browns, remove from pan and set aside.

3 Sauté garlic lightly for 30 seconds. Add capsicum and fry for a further minute, then add tomatoes. Season to taste and simmer for 10 minutes. Add eggplant and basil to the sauce and simmer for 2 minutes. Check seasoning then set aside to keep warm.

4 Cook penne in boiling salted water until *al dente*. Drain and stir through sauce with pecorino.

SERVES 4

≈ **USING QUALITY INGREDIENTS**

As with many recipes where there are few ingredients, the quality of these ingredients makes the difference between a mediocre dish and an exceptional one. Choose the best Parmesan available, and grate it just before use.

PENNE WITH LEEKS, SPINACH AND PIMIENTOS

Mellow but fresh-flavoured, this dish can be served as a first course or for a light luncheon followed by cheese and fruit. It is inexpensive, easy and can be made more glamorous simply by adding sliced prosciutto, prawns or perhaps sautéed fresh tuna.

3 large leeks, trimmed

350 g English spinach

60 g butter

1 small onion, finely chopped

salt and freshly ground black pepper

½ large pimiento (piece approximately 8 x 4 cm), cut into thin strips

300 g penne

freshly grated Parmesan cheese

1 Slice leeks thinly, using all the whites and most of the greens. Discard spinach stalks and slice leaves thinly.

2 Heat butter in a large pan and gently sauté onion for 4 to 5 minutes. Add leeks and spinach, season well, then cook over a low heat for 10 to 15 minutes. Stir through the pimiento for the last 5 minutes. Adjust seasoning to taste.

3 Cook penne in boiling salted water until *al dente* . Drain and transfer to a warm bowl. Top with the vegetable sauce and a sprinkling of Parmesan. Serve with extra Parmesan handed around.

SERVES 4

Penne with Leeks, Spinach and Pimientos

MUSHROOM AND SPINACH LASAGNE

9 dried spinach lasagne sheets or fresh spinach pasta as follows

SPINACH LASAGNE

250 g frozen spinach, thawed

2 eggs

2½ cups (300 g) plain flour or 1½ cups (200 g) flour and ½ cup (100 g) semolina

½ teaspoon salt

pinch each white pepper and ground nutmeg

SAUCE

50 g butter

450 g button mushrooms, thinly sliced

2 cloves garlic, crushed

¼ teaspoon ground nutmeg

salt and freshly ground black pepper

1 teaspoon fresh lemon juice

2½ tablespoons plain flour

3 cups (750 ml) milk

RICOTTA MIXTURE

500 g ricotta cheese

1 small egg, beaten

3 tablespoons finely chopped fresh parsley

60 g Parmesan cheese, grated

250 g mozzarella cheese, shredded

1 TO PREPARE SPINACH LASAGNE: Put spinach in a tea-towel and wring it out thoroughly to remove all excess water. Purée in a food processor or blender with 1 egg.

2 Stir flours and seasonings together, then form a well in the centre. Break the second egg into the well and beat it with a fork for seven or eight strokes before beginning to incorporate the flour. When the mixture becomes dry, add puréed spinach and work this into the flour. Continue until dough becomes sticky and difficult to work with the fork, then begin to knead by hand using extra flour as needed to form a smooth and elastic ball. Rest dough for at least 20 minutes. This whole step can be done in a food processor if preferred.

3 Divide dough into three or four balls and cover them with a plastic sheet or cloth. Roll each ball into an even thin sheet, using a hand-cranked pasta machine, or by hand with a rolling pin. Rest the sheets before trimming them into workable sizes for cooking.

4 In a large pan of boiling salted water cook the lasagne sheets in batches for 1 minute. Remove with a slotted spoon and drain on tea towels before proceeding. If using dried pasta, cook to desired degree, according to the directions on the packet. Drain as above.

5 Preheat oven to 180°C (350°F).

6 TO PREPARE SAUCE: Melt butter in a large saucepan and add mushrooms, garlic, nutmeg, salt and pepper. Stir through, then add lemon juice. Sauté for 2 to 3 minutes; do not brown. Stir in flour, cook for half a minute, then slowly add milk. Cook, stirring, until thickened into a smooth sauce.

7 TO PREPARE RICOTTA MIXTURE: In a small bowl combine ricotta, egg, half the parsley and most of the Parmesan.

8 Grease a large ovenproof dish and line it with some of the pasta sheets, bringing them up the sides and flapping out over the dish's rim; this will form an outer case for the lasagne. Cover with one-third of the ricotta mixture, one-third of the mozzarella and one-third of the mushroom sauce. Put in another layer of pasta, just as wide as the dish this time, and continue the sequence of layering, ending with the last of the mushroom sauce on top. Sprinkle with the remaining parsley and Parmesan. Now fold over the pasta flaps and trim, if necessary, so that they form a 2 to 3 cm border around the lasagne.

9 Cover the dish loosely with foil and bake for 40 minutes or so. Let stand in a warm spot for 10 minutes before serving.

SERVES 8

≈ **MUSHROOM AND SPINACH LASAGNE**

This lasagne is surprisingly light and makes an excellent luncheon or late supper dish. It can be prepared beforehand and isn't as time-consuming as other lasagnes, particularly if you are able to purchase the spinach pasta sheets. It can be made using plain pasta, but the subtle mix of flavours is lessened, along with some of the visual appeal.

MACARONI, CHEESE AND EGG CAKE

500 g elbow macaroni or ziti

CHEESE SAUCE

30 g butter

2 tablespoons plain flour

2½ cups (625 ml) milk

salt, white pepper and nutmeg

150 g Cheddar cheese, grated

1½ tablespoons grated Parmesan cheese

1 teaspoon grated onion

2 teaspoons Dijon-style mustard

1½ teaspoons chopped fresh parsley

CRUST

4 tablespoons grated Parmesan cheese

4 tablespoons breadcrumbs

1 egg, beaten

250 g mozzarella cheese, grated

3 hard-boiled eggs, shelled and sliced

1 Cook macaroni in boiling salted water until *al dente*. Drain and stir through a little vegetable oil to prevent sticking.

2 TO PREPARE CHEESE SAUCE: In a small saucepan melt butter and stir in flour. Cook until smooth. Gradually stir in the milk. Cook, stirring, until sauce begins to thicken. Add salt, pepper and nutmeg to taste, Cheddar, Parmesan, onion, mustard and parsley. Continue to cook until thick and smooth. In a bowl combine the pasta with cheese sauce and mix well.

3 Preheat oven to 180°C (350°F).

4 TO PREPARE CRUST: Mix Parmesan and breadcrumbs together and sprinkle some in a greased deep-sided rectangular casserole. Shake them around to coat the walls well, then turn out the excess. Pour in egg and swirl around the dish to cover breadcrumb mixture. Discard excess, then shake around a final coating of breadcrumbs and Parmesan.

5 Now layer one-third of the pasta in the bottom of the dish and cover this with one-third of the mozzarella. Place half the boiled egg slices in a single layer on top. Repeat this layering, then on the last level of eggs put the remaining pasta and finally the last of the mozzarella.

6 Bake for 20 to 30 minutes. Allow the cake to cool for 15 minutes, and then run a sharp knife around the edge to loosen it. Carefully turn out onto a warm serving plate and serve in slices

SERVES 6 TO 8

≈ **LINGUINE IN WHITE CLAM SAUCE**

Bottled or canned clams work very well here, and the sauce is just as good if you'd like to leave out the mushrooms. Clams can also be substituted by cockles or winkles.

LINGUINE IN WHITE CLAM SAUCE

300 g baby clams in brine, bottled or canned

1 cup (250 ml) milk

2 tablespoons olive oil

30 g butter

1 clove garlic, crushed

1 small onion, finely chopped

100 g button mushrooms, sliced

½ cup (125 ml) dry white wine

1 tablespoon finely chopped fresh parsley

½ tablespoon finely chopped fresh basil,

1 teaspoon finely chopped fresh oregano or ¼ teaspoon dried

salt and white pepper

400 g fresh linguine or 300 g dried

4 sprigs fresh basil, to garnish

1 Lightly drain clams and soak in milk for 1 to 1½ hours. Drain again, reserving ½ cup (125 ml) of the liquid.

2 Heat oil and butter in a large pot and gently sauté garlic and onion until soft. Add mushrooms, sauté briefly, and then pour in wine. Cook over medium heat to evaporate slightly, then add the herbs, clams and clam milk. Season well and cook until the sauce thickens somewhat.

3 Cook linguine in boiling salted water until *al dente*. Drain and transfer to a heated serving dish. Pour on the sauce and decorate with sprigs of basil.

SERVES 4

PUMPKIN GNOCCHI

1 kg pumpkin, skin left on

⅓ cup (50 g) semolina

⅓ to ⅔ cup (50 to 100 g) potato flour

salt, white pepper and ground nutmeg

100 g unsalted butter

freshly grated Parmesan cheese

1 Preheat oven to 180°C (350°F).

2 Cut pumpkin into pieces. Place in a shallow baking dish, skin side up, pour in 3 tablespoons water and bake until tender.

3 Remove from the oven and cool. Peel off the skin and any burnt surfaces, then mash the flesh or put it through a food mill to yield 2 cups pulp. (It's not recommended to use a blender or food processor, as the purée resulting tends to be watery and lacks body.)

4 Put pumpkin in a large bowl, season and begin to work in the flours. Use all the semolina and as much of the potato flour as gives a soft kneadable dough. Add salt, pepper and nutmeg. Knead lightly until elastic. Rest for 10 minutes.

5 Break off little pieces about 2 cm long. Roll them quickly between the fingers to obtain a smoother surface, then press them with the thumb against the curved back of a fork or grater to get the traditional gnocchi shape. Dust lightly with potato flour and rest for 10 to 12 minutes.

6 Melt butter in a saucepan and cook it over a medium heat until golden brown. Keep warm.

7 Cook the gnocchi, a few at a time, in boiling salted water. When they rise to the surface remove with a slotted spoon and transfer to warm bowls. Pour the butter over the top, sprinkle on some Parmesan and serve immediately. Extra Parmesan can be served separately.

SERVES 4

≈ **PUMPKIN GNOCCHI**

Choose firm, richly-coloured pumpkin for good texture and flavour, and work quickly and lightly with the dough to avoid toughness. If you are busy it is possible to boil the pumpkin instead of baking it, but the flavour won't be as intense, nor the texture as firm.

Preparing Pumpkin Gnocchi with brown butter and Parmesan

≈ **CRISP CHIPS**

When frying the chips, don't overcook them. They should look crisp and golden and covered in blisters.

SPINACH CHIPS

500 g frozen spinach, thawed

1⅔ cups (300 g) semolina

2 eggs

1 teaspoon vegetable oil

1 tablespoon salt

3 tablespoons grated Parmesan cheese

1 teaspoon freshly ground black pepper

1 teaspoon dried oregano

1 teaspoon onion salt

1 teaspoon garlic salt

vegetable oil for frying

1 Put spinach in a tea-towel and wring it thoroughly dry. Blend in a food processor with all the remaining ingredients except frying oil. Blend until a smooth ball of dough forms which stops the machine. If mixing by hand, chop spinach finely first.

2 Knead dough (incorporating some flour if necessary to give a dry but pliable consistency), until dough is smooth and elastic, about 6 minutes. Cover with a damp cloth or plastic and rest for 30 minutes.

3 Divide the ball into four and roll each out very thinly, using a rolling pin or pasta machine. Sprinkle each sheet lightly with flour and let rest for a further 15 minutes. Using a sharp knife or a pastry cutting wheel, cut the sheets into rectangles of about 5 x 2 cm.

4 Heat frying oil to 185°C (365°F), or until a slight haze is visible. Toss in one or two chips to check that the temperature is right, then fry them quickly in batches. It should take 5 to 10 seconds if deep-frying, or 5 to 8 seconds each side if shallow-frying. Remove with a slotted spoon and drain on absorbent paper before cooling.

MAKES ABOUT 100

Spinach Chips

RICOTTA AND SALAMI IN WINE PASTA

PASTA

2½ cups (300 g) plain flour

large pinch salt

large pinch caster sugar

1 egg, beaten

½ cup (125 ml) dry white wine, or more if needed

FILLING

250 g ricotta cheese

1 egg

100 g smoked mozzarella, finely diced

70 g lean salami, finely diced

¾ tablespoon grated Parmesan cheese

¼ teaspoon freshly ground black pepper

2 tablespoons dried breadcrumbs

1 tablespoon finely chopped fresh mint

beaten egg for sealing

vegetable oil for frying

1 TO PREPARE PASTA: Pile flour, salt and sugar on a work surface and make a well in the centre. Add egg and wine, and begin incorporating dry ingredients with a fork. When a rough dough is formed, begin kneading, adding more flour or wine to make it pliable but dry to the touch. Knead for at least 6 minutes, or until smooth and elastic. Cover with a damp cloth or plastic and rest for 30 minutes. Divide into three and roll each out to a very thin sheet. Cover and let rest for 15 minutes before cutting.

2 TO PREPARE FILLING: Combine all ingredients in a bowl and mix well.

3 Cut pasta circles 10 to 12 cm in diameter. Paint their rims with egg, then place 2 teaspoons filling along the centres. Fold over to form a half-moon shape and press edges together. Cut around the rims with a zig-zag pastry wheel or a crimper cutter and set aside in a single layer until ready to cook.

4 Heat vegetable oil in a deep-frying pan until a slight haze is visible. Fry pastries, two or three at a time, until golden and crisp on both sides. Remove with a slotted spoon and drain on absorbent paper before serving.

SERVES 3 TO 4

HAM AND MUSHROOM LASAGNE

2 tablespoons olive oil

1 small onion, finely chopped

250 g button mushrooms, sliced

800 g canned Italian peeled tomatoes, drained and finely chopped

3 tablespoons chopped fresh parsley

dry white wine

salt and freshly ground black pepper

500 g fresh lasagne sheets or 300 g packet lasagne

toasted fresh breadcrumbs

350 g unsmoked ham, cut into strips

200 g mozzarella, shredded

2 hard-boiled eggs, thinly sliced

1 In a large pan heat oil and gently sauté onion until soft. Add mushrooms and sauté briefly. Add tomatoes and parsley. Cook, covered, for 40 minutes, adding a little wine if the sauce becomes dry. Season lightly.

2 Preheat oven to 190°C (375°F).

3 Cook the lasagne sheets, a few at a time, in boiling salted water until *al dente*. Remove with a large flat slotted spoon or a skimmer and place on dry tea-towels to drain.

4 Grease a deep rectangular ovenproof dish and toss breadcrumbs in it to coat the sides. Discard any surplus.

5 Place a layer of pasta over the bottom and right up the sides. Spoon in one-third of the sauce, cover with a layer of ham, then one-third of the mozzarella, then layer half the egg slices on top. Cover these with a layer of pasta, half the remaining sauce, and continue the layers until the last is the remaining mozzarella. Fold over the top any pasta from the sides which may be exposed.

6 Bake for 30 minutes. Let sit for 3 to 4 minutes in a warm spot before serving.

SERVES 4 TO 6

≈ **WINE PASTA**

Pasta made with white wine and a touch of sugar has a flavour reminiscent of yeast dough. If the sugar is left out, the pasta, cut into shapes or ribbons, can be served with a sauce. You can substitute Bruder Basil cheese for the smoked mozzarella in this recipe.

≈ **HAM AND MUSHROOM LASAGNE**

This is a deep-flavoured lasagne which can be served as an entrée or as the main meal. Made without a white sauce, it makes a less rich dish than other lasagne, and eliminates a time-consuming step. It can be prepared up to 24 hours in advance and kept in the refrigerator until needed.

FAST PASTA

This is what pasta is all about in today's kitchen: a filling meal ready in the time it takes to cook the fettuccine or spaghetti, and one which you have prepared yourself, easily and without fuss. Because the cooking time is brief, the nutritional content of the ingredients is not lost and there's the added bonus that often there is very little washing up.

TOMATO TAGLIERINI WITH FENNEL SAUCE

2 large fennel bulbs

400 g fresh tomato taglierini

60 g butter

3 tablespoons olive oil

1 clove garlic, crushed

½ cup (125 ml) dry white wine

250 g button mushrooms, sliced

salt and white pepper

⅓ cup (80 ml) cream

2 teaspoons finely chopped fresh parsley

2 tablespoons coarsely grated
Parmesan cheese

1 Trim fennel bulbs and parboil them. Discard any tough outer stalks and then slice them thinly.
2 Cook taglierini in boiling salted water until *al dente*.
3 Heat butter and oil together in a frying pan and stir in garlic. Add fennel and white wine. Cook for 1 to 2 minutes, then add mushrooms and season with salt and pepper to taste. Add cream and parsley and cook for 30 seconds more. Stir through Parmesan.
4 Toss sauce through cooked and drained pasta and serve with extra grated Parmesan.
SERVES 4

GORGONZOLA AND PISTACHIO FETTUCCINE

The secret of this recipe is to move quickly once the Gorgonzola has been added, to avoid the cheese separating.

250 g dried fettuccine or 350 g fresh

30 g butter

2 tablespoons olive oil

1 clove garlic

2 tablespoons finely chopped fresh parsley

50 g shelled pistachio kernels

100 g milk Gorgonzola or other creamy blue cheese, e.g. Castello

2 tablespoons grated Parmesan cheese

1 Cook the fettuccine in boiling salted water until *al dente*.

2 Heat butter and oil in a pan and sauté garlic. Stir through parsley and pistachios. Cook, stirring, for 2 minutes. Remove garlic clove. Add crumbled blue cheese and stir until melted. Mix 2 tablespoons pasta water into the sauce.

3 When pasta is cooked, drain. Stir sauce and Parmesan through fettuccine and serve with extra grated Parmesan.

SERVES 4 AS AN ENTRÉE

TORTELLINI VERDI WITH RICOTTA AND PISTACHIO NUTS

500 g spinach tortellini with ricotta filling

150 g ricotta cheese

3 tablespoons grated Parmesan cheese

2 tablespoons cream

2 eggs

salt and white pepper

12 pistachio kernels, roughly chopped

1 Begin cooking tortellini.

2 In a blender or food processor combine ricotta, Parmesan and cream and mix until smooth. Transfer to a saucepan and set over a pot of boiling water. Stir occasionally while heating through.

3 Beat eggs with some salt and pepper.

4 When tortellini are cooked, drain and quickly toss through the egg mixture and the sauce. Decorate with pistachios and serve with extra grated Parmesan.

SERVES 6 AS AN ENTRÉE

CONCHIGLIE WITH SPINACH AND ALMOND SAUCE

250 g small dried conchiglie or 350 g fresh

250 g drained cooked English spinach, fresh or frozen

1 tablespoon chopped fresh basil or 1 teaspoon dried

5 tablespoons roughly chopped fresh parsley

90 g pecorino cheese, grated

½ cup (90 g) blanched almonds

2 cloves garlic, chopped

60 g butter, softened

¼ cup (60 ml) extra virgin olive oil

grated pecorino or grated pepato, extra, to serve

1 Cook conchiglie in boiling salted water until *al dente*.

2 Place all ingredients in a blender or food processor and blend to a smooth paste. Take 4 tablespoons of the pasta cooking water and blend into the sauce.

3 Drain cooked pasta and stir sauce through it. Serve with extra grated pecorino, or grated pepato for added oomph.

SERVES 4 AS AN ENTRÉE OR LIGHT MEAL

≈ **SPINACH AND ALMOND SAUCE**
The beautiful colour and good coating quality of this sauce make it very versatile. You can toss in some diced feta cheese, or some crisp bacon pieces or serve the dish in smaller portions as an accompaniment to grilled or poached fish.

Ingredients for Gorgonzola and Pistachio Fettuccine

*Pasta can be precooked
and stored and reheated
successfully if it is made
from durum wheat
semolina. Before freezing
or refrigerating, coat
pasta with a light oil,
cool and stir often to
prevent sticking. Seal it
well in a bowl before
storing. Before using,
remove and let it defrost
in the normal part of the
refrigerator.
Reheat pasta by stirring
it through a hot sauce or
cover it with a damp
cloth and place in a
preheated oven.*

≈ SPAGHETTINI
WITH ZUCCHINI
AND WALNUTS

*This can be varied by
using yellow zucchini
(courgettes) and replacing
the spaghettini with
spinach spaghetti or
fettuccine.*

ZUCCHINI WITH SAFFRON SAUCE

400 g penne or orecchiette

2 tablespoons vegetable oil

2 cloves garlic, crushed

600 g small young zucchini (courgettes), sliced in 0.5 cm rounds

salt, pepper and nutmeg

⅔ cup (160 ml) cream

1 g pure saffron powder or ¼ teaspoon saffron strands

grated Parmesan cheese, to serve

1 Cook penne in boiling salted water until *al dente*.

2 Heat oil in a large frying pan and sauté garlic and zucchini until golden brown but still crisp. Add salt, pepper and nutmeg to taste.

3 Meanwhile bring cream and saffron to the boil. Simmer gently until cream is slightly thickened and a mellow saffron colour.

4 Reserve a few slices of zucchini for decoration. Drain cooked pasta and add to the zucchini pan with saffron cream. Stir to coat well.

5 Garnish with reserved zucchini. Serve grated Parmesan separately.

SERVES 4 AS A MAIN COURSE

SPAGHETTINI WITH ZUCCHINI AND WALNUTS

400 g fresh spaghettini or 300 g dried

¼ cup (60 ml) olive oil

½ small onion, finely chopped

1 clove garlic, crushed

1 cup (100 g) walnut halves, chopped

4 small zucchini (courgettes), grated

2 tablespoons finely chopped fresh parsley

2 teaspoons chopped fresh basil or ½ teaspoon dried

salt and freshly ground black pepper

pinch nutmeg

80 g butter

3 tablespoons freshly grated Parmesan cheese

1 Begin cooking spaghettini in boiling salted water.

2 Heat oil in a large frying pan and gently sauté onion and garlic until soft. Add walnuts and sauté until slightly coloured.

3 Add zucchini, parsley and basil and cook, stirring, for 20 seconds. Season to taste with salt, pepper and nutmeg. Add butter and cook until butter is bubbling.

4 When pasta is *al dente*, drain and add to sauce. Add Parmesan and toss to coat before serving.

SERVES 4 AS AN ENTRÉE

FETTUCCINE WITH RICOTTA AND DILL SAUCE

400 g fresh wholemeal fettuccine or 300 g dried

1 clove garlic, crushed

500 g ricotta cheese

1½ cups (375 ml) milk

1½ teaspoons salt

pinch each white pepper and cayenne pepper

pinch chilli powder

½ red capsicum (pepper), chopped

2 tablespoons chopped fresh dill

1 Cook fettuccine in boiling salted water until *al dente*.

2 In a blender or food processor blend garlic, ricotta, milk, salt, peppers and chilli to form a smooth sauce. Transfer to a bowl and stir through capsicum and dill.

3 When pasta is *al dente*, mix 1 to 2 tablespoons cooking water through the sauce, then drain pasta. Add sauce to pasta and stir to coat before serving.

SERVES 4

VERMICELLI WITH WALNUT SAUCE

This dish goes very well before a main meal of fish or poultry. The rich, crunchy sauce keeps well in the refrigerator for up to 4 days, and it is also good served as a dip with crudités.

350 g fresh vermicelli or 250 g dried

1¼ cups (125 g) fresh walnut halves

1 large bunch fresh parsley, roughly chopped (to make 2 cups)

4 tablespoons fresh or dried breadcrumbs

90 g butter, softened

½ cup (125 ml) good olive oil

3 tablespoons cream

salt and white pepper

1 Begin cooking pasta in boiling salted water.

2 Place walnuts, parsley and breadcrumbs in a food processor or blender and chop until finely ground. Add butter and oil and blend again to form a thick green paste.

3 Finally, add cream and season to taste with salt and pepper. Blend to combine.

4 Drain cooked pasta and transfer to a warm serving dish. Toss through sauce and serve immediately. It is not usual to serve cheese with this dish.

SERVES 4 AS AN ENTRÉE

Walnut Sauce

VILLA ITALIANA

GNOCCHI WITH FONTINA SAUCE

200 g fontina cheese, grated or finely chopped

½ cup (125 ml) cream

80 g butter

20 g Parmesan cheese, grated

400 g gnocchi dumplings

few leaves fresh sage, to garnish

1 Place fontina, cream, butter and Parmesan in a bowl or saucepan over another saucepan of simmering water. Heat, stirring occasionally, until the cheeses have melted and the sauce is smooth and hot.

2 In the meantime start boiling water for the gnocchi, and when the sauce is about halfway done, put in the gnocchi. Drain cooked gnocchi and coat with a little vegetable oil.

3 Serve with sauce poured over gnocchi. Garnish with sage leaves sprinkled on top.

SERVES 4

BAKED PASTA WITH ZUCCHINI AND MOZZARELLA

300 g shaped pasta (fusilli, orecchiette or conchiglie)

¼ cup (60 ml) olive oil

5 small young zucchini (courgettes), cut into 1 cm rounds

salt and freshly ground black pepper

400 g canned Italian peeled tomatoes, drained and pulped

8 to 10 black olives, stoned and sliced

2 tablespoons freshly grated Parmesan cheese

1 teaspoon fresh rosemary sprigs

250 g mozzarella cheese, cut into 1 cm cubes

1 Cook pasta in boiling salted water.

2 In a large frying pan, heat oil and sauté zucchini until lightly browned, about 5 minutes. Season with salt and pepper and transfer to an oiled shallow casserole dish.

3 Preheat oven to 180°C (350°F).

4 When pasta is almost cooked, drain and add to zucchini. Add tomatoes, olives Parmesan, rosemary and one-third of the mozzarella. Sprinkle with a little more salt and pepper if desired and then toss the lot together gently.

5 Cover with remaining mozzarella and bake until cheese is melted and the top slightly browned, about 15 minutes.

SERVES 4

TAGLIERINI WITH DRIED TOMATOES AND SNOW PEAS

350 g fresh taglierini or 250 g dried

⅓ cup (80 ml) extra virgin olive oil

3 or 4 cloves garlic, crushed

1 tablespoon finely chopped fresh mint

1 tablespoon finely chopped fresh parsley

12 to 15 small snow peas (mangetout), sliced diagonally into three

10 to 12 dried tomatoes, rinsed, drained and sliced thinly

juice ½ lemon

salt and freshly ground black pepper

1 Begin cooking taglierini in boiling salted water.

2 Heat oil and very gently sauté garlic and herbs for 1 to 2 minutes. Don't have the heat so high that the oil splatters. Add snow peas and toss for 1 minute, and then stir in dried tomatoes. Add lemon juice, and season to taste with salt and pepper .

3 Drain cooked taglierini and stir it into the pan with the vegetables. Toss well.

SERVES 4

≈ **GNOCCHI WITH FONTINA SAUCE**

Fresh sage and cheese have an affinity that gives a subtle flavour hard to duplicate with dried sage. So if fresh sage is not available, try adding a different flavour, such as julienned red capsicum or thin strips of drained dried tomatoes stirred through the sauce just before serving.

≈ **TAGLIERINI WITH DRIED TOMATOES AND SNOW PEAS**

There is no substitute for dried tomatoes. If unavailable, leave them out of the recipe. It will of course taste different.

Gnocchi with Fontina Sauce

TUNA, OLIVE AND CAPER SAUCE

375 g canned tuna in brine

40 g butter

2 tablespoons plain flour

1 cup (250 ml) milk

salt and white pepper

2 teaspoons chopped fresh parsley

2 teaspoons chopped chives

juice ½ lemon

12 black olives, stoned and sliced

2 teaspoons capers, lightly chopped if large

4 to 5 drops Tabasco sauce

1 Drain tuna and reserve brine. Melt butter in a large saucepan and add flour. Cook, stirring, until smooth and golden. Add milk and reserved brine and gradually stir to a thick, smooth sauce.

2 Season to taste with salt and pepper and stir in parsley and chives. Add lemon juice, olives, capers and Tabasco sauce; stir well. Break up tuna into smaller chunks and add to sauce; cook to heat through.

SERVES 4

≈ BUYING AND USING SCALLOPS

Scallops should have creamy white meat and roe intact. They should be firm with a pleasant smell. If buying them in the shell, shells should be closed. Scallop meat can be stored in the refrigerator for up to 3 days in an airtight container.

Before cooking, remove the brown vein. You don't need to remove the roe.

TAGLIATELLE WITH SCALLOPS AND SMOKED SALMON

40 g unsalted butter

1 clove garlic, crushed

1 tablespoon grated onion

16 small scallops, cleaned and soaked in milk for 30 minutes

400 g fresh tagliatelle or 300 g dried

⅔ cup (160 ml) dry white wine

2 teaspoons finely chopped fresh parsley

salt and white pepper

⅔ cup (160 ml) cream

100 g smoked salmon, julienned

1 Heat butter and gently sauté garlic clove and onion for 1 to 2 minutes. Add drained scallops and quickly fry until opaque.

2 Put tagliatelle on to cook in boiling salted water.

3 Add wine and parsley to scallops and over a high heat reduce juices by half. Season to taste, then stir in cream. Lower the heat and cook to slightly thicken the cream.

4 Drain tagliatelle when *al dente* and transfer to a warm serving dish. Pour on sauce, add smoked salmon and toss quickly before serving.

SERVES 4 AS AN ENTRÉE

ROTELLI WITH SPINACH AND ANCHOVIES

350 g fresh rotelli or 280 g dried

50 g butter

3 cloves garlic, crushed

8 anchovy fillets, finely chopped

400 g chopped, cooked and drained spinach, fresh or frozen

800 g canned Italian peeled tomatoes, drained

4 tablespoons pine nuts, toasted

1 Cook rotelli in boiling salted water until *al dente*.

2 Melt butter in a large frying pan and sauté garlic gently for 30 seconds. Stir in anchovies and cook for another 30 seconds. Add spinach and cook to evaporate any remaining moisture; the mixture should be quite dry at this stage.

3 Break up tomatoes in your hand over the sink, shaking off excess juice, and then add pulp to spinach in the pan.

4 Drain cooked pasta lightly so that some cooking water remains, and then stir it through spinach mixture with pine nuts. Toss all together well before serving. It is not recommended to serve cheese with this dish.

SERVES 4 AS AN ENTRÉE

SEAFOOD WITH FRESH TAGLIATELLE

Very easy and very quick, this dish requires fresh pasta (preferably made from durum wheat semolina) to enable fast cooking in the final step. The result is a deliciously fresh combination of flavours.

⅓ cup (80 ml) olive oil

2 cloves garlic, crushed

500 g lobster cut into pieces with shells left on

500 g prawns (shrimps), shelled and deveined with tails left on

300 g white fish fillets, cut into pieces

2 large tomatoes, peeled, seeded and chopped

120 g red pimientos, chopped

1 teaspoon paprika

1 g pure saffron powder

salt

4 cups (1 litre) light fish stock

800 g fresh egg tagliatelle

1 In a large frying pan heat oil and add garlic. Sauté briefly and add seafood. Cook, stirring, until well coated with garlic oil.

2 Add tomatoes, pimientos, paprika, saffron and salt to taste. Pour in stock and bring to the boil. Add tagliatelle, stir in and simmer until *al dente*, 1 to 3 minutes. If it looks as though there will be excess juice left, increase the heat for the last half minute.

3 The dish is ready when the pasta is cooked. Take the pan to the table and serve immediately.

SERVES 6 TO 8

Seafood with Fresh Tagliatelle

≈ PREPARING PRAWNS

Cut off the head and remove the shell. The tail doesn't have to be removed. Use a sharp knife to slit the centre and back and pull the vein out.

TORTELLINI WITH SAUSAGE

400 g meat tortellini

20 g butter

½ green capsicum (pepper), sliced

3 good quality sausages, preferably spicy, cut in 2 cm pieces

200 g ricotta cheese

50 g pecorino cheese, grated

salt and freshly ground black pepper

1 Cook tortellini on in boiling salted water.

2 Melt butter and sauté capsicum and sausages until sausages are browned and cooked through. Keep warm.

3 In a bowl combine ricotta and pecorino, a little salt and generous grindings of black pepper. Just before serving, beat through 1 to 2 tablespoons boiling pasta water.

4 Drain tortellini and transfer to a warm serving dish. Add ricotta and sausage mixtures and toss to distribute evenly.

SERVES 4

≈ **COOKING WITH LIVER**

Young calf's liver can be used instead of lamb's but either way cook only when ready to eat; liver reheated becomes dry, tough and sharply flavoured.

PAPPARDELLE WITH LAMB'S LIVER AND BACON

400 g fresh pappardelle or 300 g dried

40 g butter

1 clove garlic

1 small onion, thinly sliced

100 g bacon, sliced into short strips

1½ teaspoons chopped fresh sage or ½ teaspoon dried

300 g lamb's liver, cleaned and sliced into strips

3 tablespoons vermouth

1 tablespoon tomato purée or the juice from a can of Italian peeled tomatoes

salt and freshly ground black pepper

1 Begin cooking pappardelle in boiling salted water.

2 Melt butter in a large frying pan and gently sauté garlic clove and onion until soft; do not brown.

3 Add bacon and sauté until crisp, and then add sage and liver. Increase heat slightly and sauté until liver is just brown.

4 Remove garlic clove and add vermouth and tomato purée; reduce. Season to taste, and add a little stock or extra tomato purée if it is drying out.

5 When the pasta is *al dente*, drain, and stir into sauce before serving.

SERVES 4 AS AN ENTRÉE OR LIGHT MAIN MEAL

LASAGNETTE WITH CHICKEN LIVERS

250 g small young stringless green beans, topped and tailed

400 g lasagnette

1½ tablespoons walnut oil

30 g butter

300 g chicken livers, cleaned, trimmed and cut in half

100 g button mushrooms, sliced

1 teaspoon balsamic vinegar or 3 teaspoons sherry vinegar

salt and white pepper

½ cup (125 ml) chicken stock

1 tablespoon roughly torn fresh Italian parsley leaves

5 to 6 walnut halves, roughly chopped (optional)

1 In a large pot of boiling water, blanch beans for 1 minute. Remove with a slotted spoon and rinse under cold water; drain. Add lasagnette to the boiling water with a pinch of salt and cook until *al dente*; drain.

2 Meanwhile, heat oil and butter in a large frying pan and add livers. Sauté quickly until browned on the outside but pink and juicy inside. Toss mushrooms through, then add vinegar. Increase heat slightly and reduce juices.

3 Season to taste, then pour in stock and quickly reduce by half. Toss in beans and lasagnette and stir in parsley. Serve on warm plates decorated with walnuts.

SERVES 4

SMOKED TURKEY AND GNOCCHI SALAD

130 g dried gnocchi shapes, not the dumplings

2 tablespoons olive oil

250 g smoked turkey, flaked into pieces 3 to 4 cm long

50 g button mushrooms, sliced

1 tablespoon chopped fresh chives

freshly ground black pepper

1 teaspoon balsamic vinegar

2 teaspoons extra virgin olive oil

2 small avocados or 1 large, quartered and sliced

100 g natural smoked cheese (e.g. smoked mozzarella or Bruder Basil) cut into 1 cm cubes

1 Cook pasta in boiling salted water until *al dente*. Drain, and rinse in cold water. Drain again and set aside.

2 Heat olive oil in a large frying pan and sauté turkey pieces, mushrooms and chives until turkey is lightly browned. Season well with black pepper. Add vinegar and olive oil and cook, stirring, until the juices have reduced and thickened. Season again. Add pasta and toss well; cook for 10 to 15 seconds.

3 Remove pan from the heat and toss in avocado slices and cheese. Stir through well to distribute the heat; then let the dish rest for 2 to 3 minutes before serving. Serve warm, or cool completely and serve at room temperature.

SERVES 4 AS AN ENTRÉE

Smoked Turkey and Gnocchi Salad

*Tomato Fettuccine
with Scallops*

TOMATO FETTUCCINE
WITH SCALLOPS

125 g unsalted butter

3 cloves garlic, crushed

150 g button mushrooms, sliced

2 tablespoons fresh lemon juice

250 g fresh scallops

**4 very small young zucchini (courgettes),
cut into 3 cm long julienne strips**

2 tablespoons finely chopped fresh parsley

salt and freshly ground black pepper

pinch cayenne pepper

500 g fresh tomato fettuccine

**2 tablespoons chopped fresh parsley,
to garnish**

1 In a large frying pan melt half the butter and sauté garlic for 1 minute; do not brown.
2 Add mushrooms and lemon juice and toss well. Add scallops with zucchini and parsley. Cover and steam gently, shaking frequently, for 1 to 2 minutes. Add remaining butter and when it's melted and blended through, salt and pepper well. Add cayenne.
3 Meanwhile, begin cooking pasta. When it is *al dente*, drain and stir through the sauce and garnish with parsley.

SERVES 4

PENNE WITH PRAWNS AND BACON

400 g penne rigate

100 g bacon, cut into narrow strips

80 g frozen peas, thawed

150 g uncooked peeled prawns (shrimps), cut in half if large

20 g butter

120 g ricotta cheese

salt and freshly ground black pepper

1 tablespoon grated Parmesan cheese

1 Cook penne in boiling salted water.

2 In a large frying pan sauté bacon until the fat melts. Add thawed peas and sauté for 1 to 2 minutes before stirring in prawns. Cook, stirring, until just done. Add butter and lower the heat so that it slowly melts.

3 In a bowl combine ricotta, salt, pepper and Parmesan. Just before serving, add 1 or 2 tablespoons boiling pasta water and whisk through. Drain penne when *al dente* and toss it through the ricotta. Then add bacon, prawns and peas and toss once more before serving.

SERVES 4

LASAGNETTE WITH MUSHROOMS AND CHICKEN

¼ cup (60 ml) milk

½ teaspoon dried tarragon or 2 teaspoons chopped fresh

400 g lasagnette

25 g butter

2 cloves garlic

200 g chicken fillet or breast, sliced

100 g button mushrooms, sliced

5 g porcini mushrooms, soaked in hot water to cover for 30 minutes then chopped (optional)

salt, pepper and nutmeg

2 cups (500 ml) cream

few sprigs fresh tarragon, for garnish

1 Put milk and tarragon in a small saucepan and bring to the boil. Remove from heat and let steep.

2 Begin cooking lasagnette in boiling salted water.

3 In a frying pan melt butter and gently sauté garlic, chicken and mushrooms until chicken is golden and cooked through. Discard garlic cloves and add chopped porcini (if used), and the strained soaking liquid. Add salt, pepper and nutmeg to taste and stir for 10 seconds or so before pouring in cream and tarragon milk. Stir well, bring to the boil and simmer until sauce thickens.

4 Drain pasta when it is *al dente* and transfer to a warm serving plate. Taste sauce for seasonings, then add to pasta and toss through. Serve decorated with tarragon.

SERVES 4

≈ **PENNE WITH PRAWNS AND BACON**

This combination appears to break all the rules — bacon with shellfish, cheese with seafood and hot with cold — but with delicious results. Cooking time is minimal and here is one instance where frozen peas are preferable to fresh, as their texture when thawed allows for a good saturation by the bacon fat.

Lasagnette with Mushrooms and Chicken

SAUCES

The secret's in the sauce, and there's no denying that it's hard to beat a delicious bowl of pasta served with your favourite sauce. The range available means that there is always a sauce that is right for the occasion. As some sauces are traditionally served as part of particular dishes, we have included whole meals here, as well as individual sauces.

PESTO GENOVESE

Pesto is traditionally served with trenette, but can go on any ribbon pasta and is very good on cheese-filled ravioli. It can be used in soups, on salads and steamed vegetables, and is perfect for drizzling over baked tomatoes. It is essential to use fresh young basil, and the sauce is at its best when a quality extra virgin olive oil is used. For variations, try pepato cheese instead of plain pecorino to give a more piquant flavour, or substitute a proportion of tender spinach leaves for some of the basil.

pinch salt (optional)
1 bunch fresh basil leaves, loosely chopped
2 cloves garlic
⅓ cup (80 ml) olive oil
¼ cup (30 g) pine nuts, lightly toasted
50 g freshly grated Parmesan cheese
50 g freshly grated pecorino cheese
½ teaspoon toasted breadcrumbs (if using food processor)

1 USING A PESTLE AND MORTAR: Add a pinch of salt to the basil, garlic, 1 tablespoon oil and a few pine nuts and begin crushing. Continue adding pine nuts and oil until you have a smooth texture. Blend in cheeses and stir well.
2 USING A FOOD PROCESSOR OR BLENDER: Add basil, garlic, breadcrumbs, pine nuts and cheeses. Chop thoroughly, and continue to blend as you gradually pour in olive oil. Continue until a mayonnaise-like texture is obtained.

SERVES 4

≈ PESTO

Pesto can be kept successfully for 5 to 7 days in the refrigerator if the surface is covered with a thin layer of olive oil, and it can be frozen if you omit the cheeses and stir them through after defrosting. However, aficionados maintain that it should be made just before needed, and that storing the sauce changes the composition of the ingredients.

Spaghetti Bolognese: Sauce from Bologna (page 53) over spaghetti

*This is another sauce
which is very versatile; it
can be served with
practically every pasta
type and it makes a good
base for the addition of
other ingredients. Try
it with smoked salmon
or prosciutto stirred
through, or a sprinkling
of caviar, or simply some
fresh sage leaves.*

Sauce of Four Cheeses

SAUCE OF FOUR CHEESES

20 g butter

1 teaspoon plain flour

¾ cup (180 ml) milk

80 g fontina cheese, shredded

80 g provolone cheese, shredded

80 g Emmenthaler cheese, shredded

80 g mozzarella cheese, shredded

freshly grated Parmesan cheese, to serve

1 Heat butter in a saucepan and when it
starts to foam, stir in flour. Cook for half a
minute and then stir in milk. Continue
cooking over a gentle heat, stirring, until
thickened and smooth. Remove from heat
and beat in all the cheeses except Parmesan.

2 Place the saucepan over a pot of boiling
water and heat until sauce is smooth,
stirring often. Don't boil once the cheeses
have been added or the sauce will separate.
Serve over hot pasta with the Parmesan
handed around separately.

SERVES 4 ENTRÉES

SORREL AND SPINACH SAUCE

250 g fresh sorrel, leaves only

200 g English spinach, leaves only

salt

40 g butter

2 tablespoons olive oil

1 tablespoon finely chopped fresh parsley

1 tablespoon finely chopped fresh basil

freshly ground black pepper

pinch ground nutmeg

⅓ cup (80 ml) cream

1 Rinse sorrel and spinach under cold water and shake off excess. Put in a large pot with a pinch of salt but no extra water and cook gently, covered, until limp and tender. Drain and chop finely.

2 Melt butter and oil in a large frying pan and add sorrel, spinach and herbs. Season with a little salt, lots of black pepper and a good pinch of nutmeg. Cook gently for 5 minutes, then add cream and simmer for 5 minutes more.

SERVES 4 TO 6

CHEESE AND NUT SAUCE

This is a good coating sauce which can be made in advance, but its success depends on using fresh walnuts (preferably just from the shell), and fresh basil. It can be served on vegetables too, and is particularly fine on green beans.

½ cup (60 g) shelled walnuts

¼ cup (30 g) pine nuts, roasted

1 teaspoon toasted fresh breadcrumbs

2 tablespoons fresh basil leaves

salt and freshly ground black pepper

1 clove garlic, crushed

2 tablespoons olive oil

1 tablespoon freshly grated Parmesan cheese

50 g ricotta cheese

1 In a food processor or blender, place nuts, breadcrumbs, basil, salt and pepper. Blend until they form a coarse paste. Add garlic and oil, and mix in.

2 Transfer to a bowl and stir through Parmesan and ricotta. Continue to mix until the sauce is smooth. Taste for salt and pepper, and add a little more Parmesan if a sharper flavour is preferred.

3 Serve over any hot pasta, mixing a tablespoon of the pasta's cooking water through first to lift the temperature and enable easier coating.

SERVES 4 ENTRÉES

'PICCHI-PACCHI'

⅓ cup (80 ml) olive oil

1 large onion, thinly sliced

1 clove garlic, crushed

4 anchovy fillets, drained and soaked in milk for 45 minutes

400 g canned Italian peeled tomatoes, drained and chopped

1 sprig fresh basil

salt and freshly ground black pepper

1 In a large pan heat oil and sauté onion and garlic until soft.

2 Add drained anchovies and cook for 1 to 2 minutes, breaking them up with the spoon as you stir.

3 Add tomatoes and basil, season lightly and simmer, covered, for 20 minutes or so until smooth and thick. Adjust seasoning. No grated cheese is served with this sauce.

SERVES 4

BAKED TOMATO SAUCE

800 g canned Italian peeled tomatoes, drained and mashed

2 cloves garlic, crushed

1 onion, finely chopped

2 teaspoons finely chopped fresh basil or 1 teaspoon dried

3 tablespoons olive oil

chilli flakes

⅓ cup (20 g) fresh breadcrumbs mixed with ⅓ cup (40 g) grated Parmesan cheese

1 Preheat oven to 200°C (400°F).

2 Put tomatoes, garlic, onion, basil and oil in an ovenproof dish and sprinkle with a few chilli flakes. Stir to combine. Sprinkle breadcrumb mixture over the top and bake uncovered for 30 minutes.

3 Don't break up the crust until the sauce is being tossed through the pasta; large crunchy bits should remain.

SERVES 4

≈ **'PICCHI-PACCHI'**

'Picchi-pacchi' is a rich, full-flavoured sauce which can be served on most types of pasta, but coming from Sicily it more often than not appears on spaghetti. There is a version which includes fried eggplant (aubergine), and another which has black olives thrown in for the last 5 minutes of cooking.

≈ **BAKED TOMATO SAUCE**

This sauce has a unique flavour that stove-top tomato sauces can't match. It can be easily adapted by adding olives, salami, sautéed vegetables, prawns or just about anything and it complements all types of pasta.

SAUCE OF LEEKS, GRUYÈRE AND CREAM

20 g unsalted butter

1 clove garlic

white of 1 large leek, thinly sliced

2 tablespoons plain flour

salt, white pepper and nutmeg

¾ cup (200 ml) milk

2 cups (500 ml) cream

100 g Gruyère cheese, grated

1 Melt butter in a saucepan and add garlic and leek. Over a low heat gently cook leek, stirring often, until golden and softened, about 8 minutes.

2 Stir in the flour and season to taste with salt, pepper and nutmeg. Cook until flour changes colour slightly.

3 Remove garlic clove and then gradually add the milk, stirring all the time. When sauce is smooth and thick, pour in cream. Bring back to the boil, lower the heat and cook for 5 minutes.

4 Add Gruyère and cook, stirring, until cheese has melted. Remove from heat and cool slightly before serving. This sauce keeps well refrigerated for up to four days.

SERVES 4

≈ **RED PESTO**

Red Pesto is a good coating sauce with an intriguing tang to it. Served over pasta shapes or ribbons, it makes a piquant first course well suited to precede a main meal of grilled or baked tuna steaks. It keeps well in the refrigerator for up to 4 days.

RED PESTO

15 g anchovy fillets, soaked in milk for 45 minutes

large pinch salt

1 clove garlic, crushed

⅓ cup (40 g) pine nuts, toasted

1 heaped tablespoon dried breadcrumbs

180 g drained, canned or bottled red pimiento, roughly chopped

50 g tomatoes, drained and seeded

2 teaspoons capers

1 teaspoon dried oregano

1 tablespoon chopped fresh parsley

2 to 3 tablespoons red wine vinegar

½ cup (125 ml) olive oil

1 In a blender or food processor blend drained anchovies, salt, garlic, pine nuts and breadcrumbs. Add pimiento and tomatoes and process until a red paste forms.

2 Add capers, oregano and parsley and blend. Add vinegar. Gradually add oil and mix until sauce is the consistency of pesto.

3 Stir through hot pasta, mixing a teaspoon of the pasta's cooking water through first, to make coating easier.

SERVES 4

SPAGHETTI ALLA PUTTANESCA

⅓ cup (80 ml) olive oil

2 cloves garlic, crushed

pinch chilli flakes

6 anchovy fillets, drained and soaked in milk for 30 minutes

400 g canned Italian peeled tomatoes

100 g black olives, sliced

1 tablespoon capers

1 sprig fresh oregano or ¼ teaspoon dried

400 g fresh spaghetti or 300 g dried

2 teaspoons chopped fresh parsley

1 Heat oil in a large frying pan and gently sauté garlic and chilli. Drain anchovies of excess milk and add to the pan, mashing them up as you stir.

2 Take the tomatoes out of the can one by one, squeezing them over the sink to remove seeds and some of the juice, before adding to the pan. Save remaining juice in the can to moisten the sauce as it is cooking. Add olives, capers and oregano and cook over a medium heat for 10 minutes.

3 Cook spaghetti in boiling salted water until *al dente*. Drain, and transfer to a warm serving dish. Pour sauce over the top and toss through parsley.

SERVES 4

MARINARA SAUCE

A marinara sauce is basically tomatoes and garlic reduced to a rich sauce. You can have an artichoke marinara, one made with olives or, of course, a seafood marinara.

¼ cup (60 ml) olive oil

2 cloves garlic, crushed

1 small onion, chopped

3 tablespoons chopped fresh parsley or half parsley and half fresh basil

6 large tomatoes, peeled, seeded and chopped or 800 g canned Italian peeled tomatoes, drained and pulped

pinch sugar

salt and freshly ground black pepper

1 In a large saucepan heat oil and sauté garlic and onion until soft and golden, about 10 minutes; do not brown.

2 Add herbs, tomatoes, sugar, salt and pepper. Simmer, stirring occasionally, until sauce is thick and mellow, about 30 minutes.

SERVES 4

PISTACHIO MAYONNAISE

3 egg yolks

1 cup (250 ml) extra virgin olive oil

salt and freshly ground black pepper

juice ½ lemon

1 tablespoon finely chopped fresh basil

2 tablespoons finely chopped fresh parsley

2 tablespoons ground pistachio nuts

1 Whisk egg yolks in a bowl. Continue to whisk and pour in oil in a very slow trickle, until it has all been absorbed. Still whisking, add salt, pepper and lemon juice to taste. Stir through basil, parsley and nuts to give a smooth, very thick sauce.

2 If the mayonnaise looks like curdling, continue its preparation to the finish. Beat another egg yolk in a clean bowl and gradually whisk in the curdled sauce. The mayonnaise will keep, covered and chilled, for up to 24 hours.

SERVES 4 TO 6

Pistachio Mayonnaise

≈ PISTACHIO MAYONNAISE

This is delicious served over hot fresh herb fettuccine or with cold shellfish and snap-peas (sugar peas) in a pasta salad. It is less successful if made with a food processor or blender. Perhaps it's the moisture in the fresh herbs being crushed that disrupts the balance of things; whatever the reason, the sauce is more likely to curdle if made with a machine and the texture and colour also suffer.

BUCATINI ALL'AMATRICIANA

This sauce from the town of Amatrice depends on a light tomato flavour and the crispness of the bacon. It used not to have much chilli at all, but as tastes changed, a hotter sauce has gradually evolved. For variations add 1 or 2 tablespoons of chopped parsley and/or some garlic, both of which nicely complement the basic ingredients.

400 g bucatini

1½ tablespoons olive oil

1 small onion, finely chopped

1 piece hot chilli or chilli flakes to taste

600 g canned Italian peeled tomatoes, drained and chopped

120 g thickly sliced pancetta or bacon, diced

2 tablespoons freshly grated Parmesan cheese

1 Begin cooking bucatini in boiling water.

2 Heat half the oil in a frying pan and sauté onion and chilli, until softened. Add tomatoes and simmer for about 7 minutes; they shouldn't be stewed into a rich sauce for this recipe.

3 Meanwhile, fry pancetta in the remaining oil until crisp. Keep warm.

4 When the pasta is *al dente*, drain and place in a warm bowl. Toss through Parmesan, sauce and lastly pancetta.

SERVES 4

≈ **FETTUCCINE WITH PEAS AND HAM IN AN EGG SAUCE**

This is also good with some sliced button mushrooms fried with the leeks.

FETTUCCINE WITH PEAS AND HAM IN EGG SAUCE

300 g fresh or frozen young peas

1 cup (250 ml) chicken stock

100 g unsalted butter

2 leeks, white part only, thinly sliced

120 g sliced ham, julienned

500 g fresh fettuccine or 380 g dried

2 medium-sized eggs

80 g Parmesan cheese, freshly grated

salt and freshly ground black pepper

1 Cook peas in chicken stock until tender. Set aside with 2 tablespoons cooking liquid.

2 Melt butter and gently fry leeks until soft and golden. Stir in peas, stock and ham. Cover and keep warm.

3 Begin cooking fettuccine in boiling salted water. While it is cooking, beat eggs with half the Parmesan and season with salt and pepper. Place in a large serving dish and keep warm.

4 When the pasta is just cooked, drain it (not too well; some water can remain) and toss immediately through egg mixture. Quickly stir in ham and pea sauce. Serve with remaining Parmesan and extra pepper.

SERVES 4 AS A LIGHT MEAL

SPAGHETTINI WITH LEMON, HAM AND CREAM

300 g dried spaghettini or 400 g fresh

80 g unsalted butter

150 g sliced strong ham, cut into thin strips

1 cup (250 ml) cream

1 tablespoon finely chopped fresh parsley

grated rind 1 lemon, the bush variety if possible

salt and freshly ground black pepper

2 tablespoons grated Parmesan cheese

1 Begin cooking spaghettini in boiling salted water.

2 Melt butter in a large deep frying pan and add ham. Cook for 30 seconds before adding the cream, parsley and lemon rind. Season with salt and pepper and cook for a further 1 to 2 minutes until thick and smooth.

3 When pasta is *al dente*, drain and add it to the pan with Parmesan. Toss quickly to coat well and heat through. Serve with additional grated Parmesan.

SERVES 4

Bucatini All'Amatriciana

≈ **PAGLIA E FIENO WITH BACON, PEAS AND MUSHROOMS**

If dried porcini can't be found, look for ceps or boletus. If reducing the amount of parsley, reduce the amount of cream also, so sauce retains the right consistency.

PAGLIA E FIENO WITH BACON, PEAS AND MUSHROOMS

200 g fresh plain fettuccine or 150 g dried

200 g fresh spinach fettuccine or 150 g dried

200 g shelled peas, fresh or frozen

200 g bacon, cut into strips, rinds reserved

6 g dried porcini mushrooms, soaked in 2 tablespoons warm water (optional)

200 g button mushrooms, sliced

1 clove garlic, crushed

1 teaspoon freshly ground black pepper

1 bunch fresh parsley, finely chopped

2¼ cups (560 ml) cream

grated Parmesan, to serve

1 Cook peas until tender in a large saucepan of boiling salted water; remove with a slotted spoon and set aside, reserving cooking liquid.

2 Fry bacon rinds in a large pot until crisp and the fat is extracted. Discard rinds and fry bacon in the fat until crisp.

3 Squeeze dried porcini over the pot, chop them finely and add to the pot with remaining soaking juice and fresh mushrooms. Stir in garlic and pepper and cook briefly. Toss in parsley and cook for 30 seconds.

4 Add cream and cook, stirring, until the sauce comes to the boil. Boil until thickened and reduced, 5 to 8 minutes.

5 Begin cooking fettuccine in the water used for the peas. When *al dente*, drain and transfer to a warm serving dish. Toss the sauce through, and serve with freshly grated Parmesan.

SERVES 4

PENNE ALL'ARRABBIATA

10 g dried porchini mushrooms (optional)

2 tablespoons olive oil

1 onion, finely chopped

2 cloves garlic, crushed

125 g pancetta or unsmoked bacon, cut into strips

600 g canned Italian peeled tomatoes, drained and chopped

¼ teaspoon chilli flakes

400 g penne

30 g pecorino cheese, grated

40 g butter, cut into slivers and kept cold

1 If using porcini, soak in 1 tablespoon water for 1 hour and then cut into thin strips. (Reserve the juice for another use.)
2 Heat oil in a large saucepan and sauté onion and garlic gently for 5 minutes. Add pancetta and sauté for a further 5 minutes.
3 Add porcini, tomatoes and chilli flakes and simmer over moderate heat until thickened and rich, 20 to 30 minutes. Taste for seasoning and add more chilli if you like. If the sauce appears to be drying out, stir in 1 to 2 tablespoons pasta cooking water.
4 Begin cooking pasta in boiling salted water and when it is just *al dente*, drain.
5 When ready to serve, toss penne and pecorino in with sauce and stir while heating through. Quickly toss through butter and serve.

SERVES 4

≈ COMBINING SAUCE AND PASTA

A step practised by a lot of Italian cooks is to unite the sauce with the pasta straight after cooking. This keeps everything hot and results in a quick and even distribution of flavours; you can save a little of the sauce for decoration, if desired. When using a cold sauce with hot pasta, for example Pesto, quickly mix a couple of tablespoons of cooking water through the sauce to help it coat more readily.

SAUCE FROM BOLOGNA

60 g butter

1 small onion, finely chopped

1 stalk celery, finely chopped

1 small carrot, finely chopped

60 g pancetta or bacon, finely chopped

1 bay leaf

300 g quality beef, minced

1½ teaspoons plain flour

½ cup (125 ml) dry red wine

15 g dried porcini mushrooms, soaked in a little warm water for 1 hour, then chopped (optional)

salt and freshly ground black pepper

pinch nutmeg or cloves

½ cup (125 ml) beef stock or consummé

½ cup (125 ml) milk

2 tablespoons cream

1 chicken liver, finely chopped

1 In a large pot melt butter and gently sauté onion, celery, carrot, pancetta and bay leaf for 8 to 10 minutes.
2 Add mince, increase the heat slightly and cook until golden brown. Sprinkle in flour, stir through and cook for 30 seconds before adding wine. Stir over a high heat until most of it is evaporated.
3 Add porcini (if used) plus the soaking liquid, and taste for salt before seasoning. Add nutmeg and half the stock and simmer over a low heat, covered for 1½ hours.
4 Stir from time to time and add remaining stock as you go. Add milk when two-thirds through and adjust seasonings. Just before serving stir in cream and chicken liver and cook, uncovered. for a final minute or two.

SERVES 4

≈ SAUCE FROM BOLOGNA

The true Bolognese sauce bears little resemblance to that which is found outside Italy; it's not even served with spaghetti, but tagliatelle, again the creation of Bologna. Like the city, the sauce is mellow and sophisticated. Its flavour comes from long gentle cooking and the addition of milk softens and sweetens it. No garlic is necessary and tomatoes aren't used, although some like to add a tablespoon or two of tomato paste (concentrated tomato purée) for extra richness and colour.

≈ SAUCE CONSISTENCY

Pasta sauces should have a good thick coating consistency, so where possible use thick, rich or double cream. For ease of access, most recipes specify single cream and will work with this but cooking time is longer. When using thick, rich or double cream, reduce cooking time slightly.

FINE FARE

A deliciously filling meal can be made with pasta of all descriptions. Serve long pasta (fettuccine, taglierini, spaghetti or linguine) with a good coating sauce based on oil, tomato, cream or soft melting cheeses. Twisted or hollow pasta (fusilli, zitoni or rotelli) is best with chunky sauces. Long fine strands (vermicelli or angel's hair) are delicious with clinging sauces made of butter and cheese, raw tomato, or an egg base and wide flat noodles like pappardelle or lasagnette go with gutsy meaty sauces.

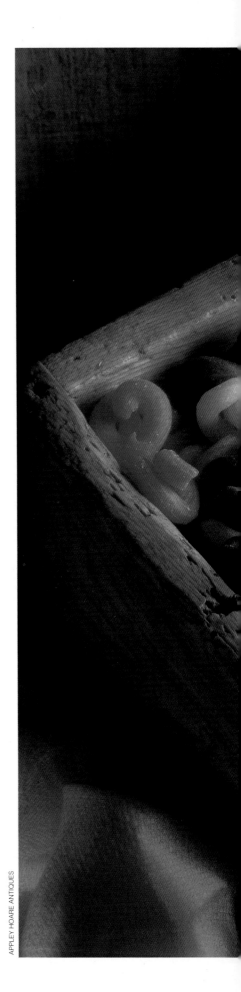

≈ COOKING FOR MANY

If you are cooking for a crowd, precook pasta in batches, then oil it lightly and keep it warm in the oven covered with a damp cloth.

FARFALLE WITH SMOKED SALMON AND MASCARPONE

300 g farfalle

2 leeks, white part only, thinly sliced

40 g butter

½ deep red capsicum (pepper), julienned

1⅔ cups (400 g) mascarpone or thickened cream

200 g smoked salmon, cut into thin strips

salt and white pepper

chopped fennel tops (optional)

1 Cook farfalle in boiling salted water until *al dente*.

2 Cook leeks gently in melted butter for a few minutes, being careful not to brown them. Reserve a few pieces of capsicum for decoration, and add the rest to the leeks. Cook for a further 30 seconds.

3 Add mascarpone and bring to the boil. Stir in most of the smoked salmon and cook just long enough to heat through. Taste for salt and add a pinch if needed. Add a pinch of pepper. Toss in the fennel tops.

4 Add to the drained pasta and decorate with reserved capsicum and salmon.

SERVES 4

PASTA AND BEAN SOUP

Pasta and beans is common to many regions where they each have their special recipes. In Venice they like their pasta and beans flavoured with a touch of cinnamon and the bone from a Parma ham; a subtle but unforgettable flavour sometimes enhanced with Parmesan cheese.

250 g borlotti beans, soaked in water overnight

1 prosciutto or ham bone

1 onion, chopped

pinch cinnamon

cayenne pepper

2 teaspoons olive oil

2 cups (500 ml) chicken stock

120 g tagliatelle, plain or spinach, broken into 3 to 4 cm lengths

Pasta and Bean Soup

1 Drain and rinse beans, cover with cold water in a saucepan and bring to the boil. Stir, then boil for 15 minutes.

2 Drain beans and transfer to a large pot with ham bone, onion, cinnamon, pinch of cayenne, olive oil and stock. Add cold water to cover. Cover pot well and simmer until beans are cooked and have begun to thicken the stock. Remove bone and cut off any meat from it. Flake this and return to the pot; discard bone.

3 Taste for seasonings; salt may be needed, depending on the bone used. Bring the soup back to the boil, then toss in pasta and cook until it is *al dente*. Let the pot sit off the heat for 1 to 2 minutes before serving.

SERVES 5 TO 6

BAKED MUSHROOM AND RICOTTA PARCELS

PASTA

1⅔ cups (200 g) plain flour

salt

2 eggs plus 2 yolks, beaten together

20 g butter, melted

1¼ cups (310 ml) milk

extra melted butter

FILLING

40 g butter

500 g button mushrooms, sliced

¼ teaspoon each salt, freshly ground black
pepper and nutmeg

2 tablespoons toasted fresh breadcrumbs

3 tablespoons finely chopped fresh parsley

400 g ricotta cheese

100 g mascarpone

1 tablespoon grated Parmesan cheese

1 egg plus 1 yolk, beaten together

TOPPING

50 g Parmesan cheese, grated

75 g butter, melted

1 **TO PREPARE PASTA:** Sift flour and a
pinch of salt into a bowl. Add beaten eggs
and butter and stir to combine. Gradually
mix in milk until a thick batter is obtained.
Continue to beat a further 7 or 8 minutes to
get a smooth consistency. Rest for at least
5 minutes.

2 Heat some of the extra butter in a small
frying pan, and then pour in enough batter
to thinly cover the bottom. Gently cook on
both sides, pancake fashion, until golden.
Remove from the pan and repeat with
remaining batter, buttering the pan as you
go. There should be 6 to 8 cooked sheets,
depending on the size of your pan. Trim each
one neatly into squares and set aside.

3 **TO PREPARE FILLING:** Heat butter in a
frying pan and fry mushrooms until golden
but still crisp. Season with salt, pepper and
nutmeg and stir in breadcrumbs and parsley.

Transfer the mixture to a bowl and mix with
ricotta, mascarpone, Parmesan and eggs.
Combine well.

4 Preheat oven to 200°C (400°F).

5 Place equal amounts of filling in the
centre of each fried pasta sheet, then fold the
corners of each over, in the manner of an
envelope, to form a parcel. Arrange these
side by side in a buttered shallow ovenproof
dish. Sprinkle the top with Parmesan and
melted butter and bake until golden, about
15 minutes.

SERVES 4

CHICKEN, LEEK AND CHICKPEA SOUP

4 cups (1 litre) chicken stock

125 g tiny pasta shapes (ditalini, tiny shells)

20 g butter

1 leek, white part only, sliced

1 clove garlic

½ cup (110 g) roasted chickpeas

1 tablespoon plain flour

2 heaped tablespoons finely chopped fresh
Italian parsley

salt and freshly ground black pepper

pinch cayenne pepper

1 cup (200 g) chopped cooked chicken meat

1 Put chicken stock in a saucepan and bring
to the boil. Add pasta and cook until barely
done. Remove with a slotted spoon, keeping
stock on the heat and just boiling.

2 Meanwhile, melt butter in a large
saucepan and gently sauté leek and garlic
until golden, not brown. Add chickpeas, toss
for a minute and then sprinkle with the
flour. Fry for 10 seconds or so, then
gradually blend in boiling stock.

3 Add parsley, salt and cayenne and a good
half dozen grinds of the pepper mill. Add
pasta and chicken meat and bring back to
the boil before serving.

SERVES 4

≈ **HEALTHY BAKED
PARCELS**

*This method of baking
filled pasta parcels is
great for the diet-
conscious, as it does away
with the need for the
coating sauce that
conventional cannelloni
require. Just be careful
not to over-bake, as this
will give a dry, tough
pasta. Make sure you
don't use too much butter
when cooking the sheets.*

≈ **CHICKEN, LEEK
AND CHICKPEA SOUP**

*The subtle flavour of
this soup can be made
even more interesting by
using fresh coriander
instead of parsley, and
frying a pinch of chilli
with the leek.*

The herb pasta, minus its filling, can be used for a stunning entrée or light meal. Simply cut it into squares and serve with a light coating sauce such as pistachio mayonnaise or pesto. Flat squares of pasta, known as quadrucci, can be any size from small pieces used in soups, to larger elegant sheets of 8 to 10 cm square to be served with a sauce.

SPICY RICOTTA AGNOLOTTI IN HERB LEAF PASTA

PASTA

2½ cups (300 g) plain flour

pinch salt

3 eggs, lightly beaten

nicely shaped leaves of any flat-leaved herb (continental parsley, chervil or coriander), reserve some for decoration

1 egg, beaten

FILLING

500 g ricotta

2 tablespoons grated Parmesan cheese

pinch grated nutmeg

pinch chilli powder

salt

approximately ½ cup (30 g) fresh breadcrumbs

TO FINISH

½ cup (125 ml) light olive oil

4 cloves garlic

freshly grated Parmesan cheese

fresh herbs

1 TO PREPARE PASTA: Mix flour and salt in a processor for a second or two. Add whole eggs and continue to process until a smooth ball forms. Incorporate more flour or a little water, if necessary. Cover dough with a damp cloth or plastic and rest for 30 minutes.

2 Divide dough into four and, working one quarter at a time, roll out until a thickness is reached which is twice that of your final pasta. You can use a long rolling pin but a more consistent result is obtained using a hand-cranked pasta machine. Do not flour the surface before the next step.

3 Take some herb leaves and discard thick or fleshy stems, then separate into attractive sections of about 1 cm each. Place at 3 to 4 cm intervals over half the pasta sheet. Fold the plain half over this and roll out.

It may be necessary to roll the pasta at this thickness several times to fully press the herb, which will take on a delicate stretched appearance.

4 Cover each sheet with a tea-towel.

5 Using a pastry cutter of 8 to 10 cm diameter, cut out circles over the herbs on the pasta sheets, keeping the finished circles covered as you work.

6 TO PREPARE FILLING: Mix first five ingredients together, then add breadcrumbs until a light but manageable texture is reached.

7 Lay out half a dozen circles, paint their edges with egg and place some filling across the centre. Fold each one over to encase filling, press edges together and trim with a zig-zag pastry wheel. Set aside, uncovered, until all are finished.

8 TO FINISH: Heat oil in a large pan or wok and gently sauté garlic over a low heat. Discard garlic and keep oil warm.

9 Cook agnolotti in boiling salted water until *al dente*. Drain, then transfer to the pan with the olive oil and toss to coat.

10 Serve immediately with a sprinkling of herb leaves and Parmesan.

SERVES 4

TAGLIATELLE WITH ZUCCHINI AND BASIL

600 g small zucchini (courgettes), cut into 4 x 1 cm sticks

70 g unsalted butter

½ cup (125 ml) vegetable oil

1 tablespoon plain flour

1 cup (250 ml) milk

400 g fresh tagliatelle or 300 g dried

½ cup (125 ml) cream

70 g fresh basil, finely chopped

1 Put zucchini sticks in a colander, sprinkle with a little salt and leave to drain for 30 minutes; pat dry with cloth.

2 Heat a little butter and oil in a large pan and fry zucchini until brown but still crisp. Remove from heat and set aside.

3 Melt rest of oil and butter in a saucepan. Add flour and cook, stirring until the paste is smooth and slightly coloured. Gradually add milk, stirring to break up any lumps. Cook until thickened and smooth.

4 Begin cooking tagliatelle in boiling salted water. Add cream to the white sauce and return to the boil. When thickened, remove from heat and stir in zucchini and basil. When the pasta is *al dente*, drain and transfer to a warm serving dish. Pour the sauce over it and serve immediately.

SERVES 4

≈ **TAGLIATELLE WITH ZUCCHINI AND BASIL**

This has a delicate balance of flavours which should not be missed when young basil is available. It is an excellent dish to precede a main course of lamb's kidneys or liver.

Tagliatelle with Zucchini and Basil

VILLA ITALIANA

Carrot-flavoured pasta has a fresh, slightly nutty flavour which can be served a number of different ways. Here, with a cream sauce it is rich and sweet.

Fresh Carrot Pasta

FRESH CARROT PASTA WITH CREAM AND MINT

PASTA

200 g carrots, peeled and diced
2 eggs
½ tablespoon vegetable oil
1½ cups (250 g) semolina
1½ cups (185 g) plain flour
1 teaspoon salt
pinch nutmeg
pinch white pepper

SAUCE

200 g carrots, peeled and julienned
40 g butter
1 tablespoon finely chopped fresh mint
1¼ cups (300 ml) cream
salt and white pepper

1 TO PREPARE PASTA: Purée carrots finely in a food processor or blender. If using a food processor, add the rest of the ingredients and process to form a dough.

2 To mix by hand, place flours and seasonings in a pile on a work surface and make a well in the centre. Add eggs, oil and carrot purée and begin working into the dry ingredients with a fork until a roughly formed dough results. Now take the dough and begin kneading by hand, incorporating extra flour if needed, to form a smooth, elastic ball. This will take 8 to 10 minutes. Cover with a damp cloth or plastic and rest for 30 minutes.

3 Divide the dough into three and, working one-third at a time, roll out to very thin sheets using a rolling pin or a hand-cranked pasta machine. Trim to rectangles approximately 20 cm long; then cover and rest for 15 minutes.

4 If cutting by hand, roll up each rectangle along its length and slice off sections about 0.5 cm in width which unroll to become taglierini. If using a pasta machine, cut to desired width. Dust the ribbons lightly with flour and let rest, uncovered, to dry slightly.

5 TO PREPARE SAUCE: Blanch carrots in boiling water until tender-crisp. In a saucepan melt butter and gently sauté mint for 30 seconds. Add cream and simmer, uncovered, to thicken. Season the sauce lightly and add the carrots. Put pasta on to cook in boiling salted water. Drain pasta when it is *al dente*, stir through a little vegetable oil and then transfer to warm plates. Pour on the sauce and serve at once.

SERVES 5 TO 6

SEAFOOD PASTA SALAD

150 g fresh fettuccine or 100 g dried (include some tomato flavoured if possible), broken into short lengths

150 g calamari (squid) rings

150 g baby clams, bottled or canned, drained

¾ cup (180 ml) milk

1 tablespoon olive oil

250 g cooked prawns (shrimps), cut in half if large

1 very small red onion, thinly sliced

1 small red capsicum (pepper), sliced

1 stalk celery, sliced

1 to 2 tablespoons chopped fresh dill

125 g cherry tomatoes, yellow or red

DRESSING

¾ cup (180 ml) olive oil

2 cloves garlic, crushed

juice 1 lemon

2 tablespoons white wine vinegar

salt and freshly ground black pepper

1 Cook pasta in boiling salted water until *al dente*. Drain, rinse under cold water and drain again. Transfer to a large serving bowl and stir through a little of the olive oil.

2 Soak calamari rings and clams in milk for at least 30 minutes, drain, and then fry them gently in 1 tablespoon olive oil until the calamari is opaque and tender. Transfer to the salad bowl.

3 Add prawns, onion, capsicum and celery and toss lightly.

4 TO PREPARE DRESSING: In a screw-top jar combine ingredients and shake well. Pour over salad. Add half the dill and toss lightly but thoroughly to coat the ingredients. Chill for 1 hour or more. When ready to serve, decorate with remaining dill and tomatoes.

SERVES 3 TO 4

PASTA SALAD WITH CHICKEN, PRAWNS AND MELON

120 g elbow macaroni or other medium-sized pasta shape

vegetable oil

300 g chicken fillets

salt and freshly ground black pepper

30 g butter

1 honeydew melon

300 g small cooked prawns (shrimps), peeled and deveined

250 g celery, finely sliced

DRESSING

2 tablespoons mayonnaise

3 tablespoons natural yoghurt

1½ tablespoons cream

¼ teaspoon chilli sauce, or to taste

1 teaspoon chopped fresh dill, plus a few sprigs to garnish

1 teaspoon gin (optional)

sugar

1 Cook pasta in boiling salted water until just *al dente*. Drain, rinse under cold water and drain again. Transfer to a salad bowl and stir through a little vegetable oil.

2 Season chicken breasts and cook them in butter until golden. Cool, then slice into strips and add to the pasta.

3 Cut out the flesh of the honeydew using a melon baller, and add these to the salad bowl along with the prawns and celery.

4 TO PREPARE DRESSING: Mix mayonnaise, yoghurt, cream, chilli sauce, dill and gin together and season to taste with salt, pepper and sugar. Pour over salad and toss lightly to coat. Cover with plastic wrap and chill for 1 hour or more before serving.

SERVES 4 TO 6

≈ **HONEYDEW MELON**

Rockmelon (cantaloupe) can be substituted for honeydew melon in this recipe.

≈ BROAD BEANS

Fresh broad beans, crisp celery, extra virgin olive oil, and Parmigiano Reggiano; add some freshly ground black pepper and lemon juice and you have a wonderful combination which can be adapted to both hot and cold pasta dishes. Fresh broad beans enjoy a very limited season. The fiddly job of shelling and peeling broad beans can be done in advance.

≈ PANCETTA

Pancetta is salted and spiced raw belly pork.

TAGLIATELLE AND BROAD BEANS

200 g shelled fresh young broad beans

1 tablespoon olive oil

2 cloves garlic

100 g pancetta or bacon, diced medium finely

400 g fresh tagliatelle or 300 g dried

1 stalk celery, sliced

1 teaspoon Dijon-style mustard

1 tablespoon finely chopped fresh parsley

salt and freshly ground black pepper

juice ½ lemon

1 tablespoon extra virgin olive oil

200 g Parmigiano Reggiano, cut into 1 cm cubes (best quality Parmesan cheese)

1 Cook beans in boiling water until *al dente*, about 2 minutes, depending on their freshness. Drain, rinse under cold water and drain again. When cool enough to handle, peel the skins off; then set aside.

2 Heat oil in a frying pan and sauté garlic cloves and pancetta until the latter is crisp and light brown.

3 Begin cooking tagliatelle in boiling salted water.

4 To the frying pan add celery, mustard, parsley, salt and pepper. Stir and cook for 1 minute. Remove garlic cloves from the pan and add broad beans, lemon juice and extra virgin olive oil. Toss to heat.

5 When pasta is *al dente* drain and add to the pan with Parmesan. Toss briefly before transferring to individual plates.

6 Serve with freshly grated Parmesan cheese and the pepper mill handed around.

SERVES 4 AS AN ENTRÉE OR LIGHT MEAL

SMOKED TROUT WITH FUSILLI

400 g fresh fusilli or 280 g dried

2 tablespoons olive oil

1½ tablespoons finely chopped leek

400 g canned Italian peeled tomatoes

large pinch nutmeg

¼ teaspoon ground black pepper

¾ cup (180 ml) cream

salt

½ cup (125 ml) brandy

200 g smoked trout fillets, sliced into 2 cm pieces

LEMON PARMESAN CRUMBS

2 tablespoons grated Parmesan cheese

2 teaspoons dried breadcrumbs

2 teaspoons finely chopped fresh parsley

rind 1 lemon, grated

1 Begin cooking fusilli in boiling salted water.

2 In a frying pan, heat oil and cook leek gently until soft but not browned, about 3 minutes. Drain tomatoes and squeeze each one in your hand over the sink to remove excess juice and most of the seeds. Continue squeezing so that the pulp breaks up, then add to the leeks in the pan. Cover and cook over a low heat for 3 to 4 minutes. Stir in nutmeg and black pepper. Add cream.

3 Cook gently for a further minute or two with the lid on. Taste for salt. Sometimes salt is not required, depending on the smoked trout.

4 Drain pasta when it is three-quarters done and add to the sauce with brandy. Now turn up the heat and cook, stirring often, until the sauce is slightly thickened. Toss in trout and stir until heated through, 20 seconds or so.

5 TO PREPARE LEMON PARMESAN CRUMBS: Combine ingredients and mix well. Hand round separately.

SERVES 4

GREEN SALAD PRIMAVERA

200 g fresh spinach fusilli, rotelli or other shape, or 150 g dried

250 g shelled fresh green peas

125 g small stringless green beans, topped, tailed and halved

200 g fresh asparagus, cut into 4 cm lengths

200 g broccoli florets

2 small zucchini (courgettes), sliced diagonally

few sprigs fresh tarragon, to garnish

DRESSING

¼ cup (60 ml) olive oil

1½ tablespoons fresh lemon juice

1 teaspoon Dijon-style mustard

1 tablespoon finely chopped fresh tarragon or ½ teaspoon dried, crumbled and steeped in 1 teaspoon olive oil for 45 minutes

salt and freshly ground black pepper

1 Cook pasta in boiling salted water until just *al dente*. Drain, rinse under cold water and drain again. Transfer to a bowl and stir through a little olive oil to prevent it sticking together.

2 Separately blanch all the vegetables until tender-crisp; drain, rinse under very cold water and drain again. Add to pasta.

3 TO PREPARE DRESSING: Combine all ingredients. Pour over the vegetables and toss lightly to coat. Decorate with tarragon sprigs. Can be served immediately, but is best if refrigerated for 1 to 2 hours first.

SERVES 5 TO 6 AS A LIGHT MEAL

Green Salad Primavera

VILLA ITALIANA

This light lasagne has a delicate flavour made possible only by using fresh basil; an interesting variation is to use the purple basil sometimes available.

Ricotta and Basil Lasagne

RICOTTA AND BASIL LASAGNE

500 g fresh lasagne sheets or 350 g dried

60 g butter

2 tablespoons plain flour

salt and white pepper

pinch nutmeg

2 cups (500 ml) milk

1 tablespoons finely chopped fresh basil

100 g ricotta cheese

50 g Parmesan cheese, grated

1 tablespoon extra chopped fresh basil

1 In a pan of boiling salted water cook the lasagne sheets, a few at a time, until *al dente*.

Take out with a slotted spoon and dry between tea-towels. It is necessary to precook the pasta sheets as the lasagne isn't in the oven long enough to steam them.

2 Melt butter in a saucepan and stir in flour. Add a little salt, pepper and nutmeg and cook over a gentle heat until it starts to change colour. Stir in milk, a little at a time, and stir until smooth and thickened. Remove from the heat and stir in 1 tablespoon basil, the ricotta and half the Parmesan. Check seasonings.

3 Preheat oven to 200°C (400°F).

4 In a greased ovenproof dish place a sheet of pasta, followed by a thin layer of ricotta mixture. Sprinkle this with some Parmesan and extra basil. Continue to layer in this order, finishing with the last of the sauce and Parmesan.

5 Bake for just 20 minutes and serve hot.

SERVES 4 TO 5 AS AN ENTRÉE

TUNA AND SPINACH ROTOLO

PASTA

2½ cups (300 g) plain flour

large pinch salt

3 eggs, beaten

FILLING

1.2 kg fresh English spinach

250 g canned tuna in olive oil, drained and flaked

6 to 8 anchovy fillets, finely chopped

50 g Parmesan cheese, grated

1 cup (60 g) fine white fresh breadcrumbs

3 eggs, beaten

salt and freshly ground black pepper

1 **TO PREPARE PASTA:** Pile flour and salt onto a work surface and make a well in the centre. Add eggs and begin to incorporate them into the flour, using a fork. When you have loosely united dough, use your hands

ACCOUTREMENT COOK SHOPS

and begin kneading, adding a little flour or water if necessary as you go. Continue until a smooth, elastic dough is obtained, about 6 minutes. Cover with a damp cloth or a sheet of plastic and rest for 30 minutes.

2 To Prepare Filling: Remove stems from spinach leaves and discard. Rinse leaves under cold water and shake off the excess. Place in a large pot with a good pinch of salt and cook, covered, over a low heat until wilted and tender. Drain and cool slightly. Squeeze out any excess water and chop spinach finely. Put in a large bowl and add tuna, anchovies, Parmesan, breadcrumbs, eggs, a little salt and lots of black pepper. Mix thoroughly.

3 To Assemble: Using a rolling pin roll out the dough to a large, even rectangle 3 to 4 mm thick. Place on a lightly floured cloth. Spread the filling over the dough, leaving 3 cm around the edges. Roll up the dough, Swiss roll fashion, using the cloth to help lift and roll smoothly. Firmly wrap the roll in a thin layer of muslin and tie off the ends securely with string. Place in a long narrow flameproof pan, cover with lightly salted cold water and bring to the boil. Lower the heat and simmer for 15 to 20 minutes. Allow the rotolo to cool slightly in the cooking water before removing. Carefully take off the cloth and cut into slices for serving.

SERVES 6

≈ **STUFFED PASTA ROLLS**

Stuffed pasta rolls can be presented in several different ways. The slices can be arranged down a long, shallow serving dish and topped with a hot light sauce such as fresh tomato; or they can be placed in a buttered ovenproof dish, sprinkled with Parmesan and butter and placed under a hot grill for 5 minutes. For a milder flavour and slightly crisper texture, pour melted butter over the uncut roll and pop into a hot oven for 4 to 5 minutes. Rotolos make an eye-catching buffet dish and are ideal served as an elegant appetiser or for a light luncheon.

PENNE AND FRESH TUNA WITH RAISIN AND ALMOND SAUCE

30 g butter
700 g fresh tuna steaks, cut into strips
300 g penne
2 egg yolks, beaten

SAUCE
90 g butter
2 tablespoons plain flour
¼ teaspoon nutmeg
salt and white pepper
1 cup (250 ml) white wine
2 tablespoons currants
⅓ cup (60 g) raisins
¼ cup (30 g) blanched almonds, slivered
1 tablespoon fresh lemon juice
1 teaspoon sugar

1 Melt butter in a large pan and gently sauté tuna until cooked through. Transfer to a plate and keep warm.

2 To Prepare Sauce: Melt butter and stir in flour. Cook, stirring, until the roux is smooth and golden. Add nutmeg, salt and pepper to taste and cook briefly. Gradually pour in wine, stirring constantly.

3 When the sauce is smooth stir in currants, raisins, almonds, lemon juice and sugar, bring to the boil and simmer over a low heat for 20 minutes.

4 Cook penne in boiling salted water.

5 Whisk a little of the hot sauce through the egg yolks, then, off the heat, whisk this mixture back into the sauce; keep warm.

6 Drain penne when it is *al dente*, and stir through a little vegetable oil; transfer to warmed plates.

7 Top the pasta with pieces of tuna, then pour over sauce and serve, allowing guests to do the tossing.

SERVES 4

≈ **PENNE AND FRESH TUNA WITH RAISIN AND ALMOND SAUCE**

Here the rich, gamey flavour of tuna is nicely balanced by dried fruit and nuts. To vary, use a white-fleshed fish such as cod or ling, and omit the currants and raisins. Double the amount of almonds and toast them in the butter before making the roux.

TOMATO FETTUCCINE WITH CALAMARI AND SNOWPEAS

A mild but rich sauce, this can be varied by omitting the cream and tossing the cooked pasta through the sauce in the pan before serving. It works as well using plain fettuccine and tossing through slivers of tomatoes at the end.

SCALLOPS AND ROASTED CAPSICUMS WITH TAGLIERINI

If time is pressing, this sauce can be made quickly by substituting canned or bottled pimientos for the roasted capsicum.

400 g fresh taglierini or 300 g dried

1 red capsicum (pepper)

1 green capsicum (pepper)

450 g fresh scallops, trimmed and cleaned

salt and freshly ground black pepper

plain flour

2 tablespoons olive oil

1 clove garlic

2 teaspoons chopped fresh parsley

juice ½ lemon

2 leeks, white part only, thinly sliced

1 cup (250 ml) chicken stock

2 tablespoons toasted fresh breadcrumbs mixed with grated rind 1 lemon

1 Roast capsicums under a hot grill until charred and blistered on all sides. Remove from heat and place in a plastic bag, tied off, to sweat. Remove when cool and peel and seed them, then slice into strips.

2 Season scallops and coat them in flour. Heat oil, add garlic and quickly sauté scallops until just brown. Remove from the pan and sprinkle with parsley and lemon juice. Remove garlic clove.

3 Add leeks to the pan and gently sauté until soft. Pour in stock, increase the heat slightly and reduce by half. Add scallops and capsicum to the leek pan and heat through.

4 Cook pasta in boiling salted water until *al dente*. Drain and add to the sauce. Stir to coat and adjust seasoning if necessary. Serve at once, sprinkled with the lemon breadcrumbs.

SERVES 4

SEAFOOD AGNOLOTTI WITH CORIANDER AND ZUCCHINI

PASTA

3¼ cups (400 g) plain flour

large pinch salt

4 eggs

FILLING

250 g white fish fillets (gemfish, ocean perch, plaice or haddock), poached, boned and finely chopped

250 g cooked prawn (shrimp) or crab meat, finely chopped

1½ tablespoons finely chopped fresh coriander

⅔ cup (40 g) fresh breadcrumbs

40 g fontina cheese, finely grated

½ teaspoon salt

60 g cooked spinach, wrung-dry and finely chopped

400 g ricotta

1 egg, beaten, to seal pasta

SAUCE

80 g butter

1 small zucchini (courgette), grated

salt and nutmeg

fresh coriander leaves, cut into thin strips, to garnish

1 TO PREPARE PASTA: Pile flour on a work surface, make a well in the centre and add salt and eggs. Using a fork, break up eggs and begin to incorporate flour. Continue blending flour until you have a loosely formed mass of dough. Begin kneading with your hands, adding more flour or a little water if needed. Knead until you have a smooth, elastic ball. Wrap in a damp cloth or plastic wrap and let rest for 30 minutes.

2 Divide the ball into four, then, using a rolling pin or a hand-cranked pasta machine, roll out each one in turn to a very thin, even sheet. Rest, covered, for 12 to 15 minutes.

3 To Prepare Filling: Combine all ingredients except beaten egg, in a bowl and mix well.

4 Using a biscuit cutter or an upturned glass, cut out circles of about 5 cm diameter from the sheets of pasta, keeping pasta and circles you are not working on covered to prevent drying out. Working a few at a time, paint around the rim of each circle with beaten egg, placing a little filling in the centre and fold over to form a half-moon shape. Press the sides together and then go round the cut edges with a zigzag pastry wheel or a crimper cutter. As the agnolotti are completed, place them in a single layer and dust very lightly with flour. Simmer the agnolotti in boiling salted water for 3 to 4 minutes.

5 To Prepare Sauce: Melt butter in a saucepan until golden, and then add zucchini. Stir over a very low heat, season with a little salt and a pinch of nutmeg, and keep warm.

6 Drain agnolotti, transfer to a warm serving dish and toss through sauce. Sprinkle with sliced coriander and toss again before serving.

Serves 4

TOMATO FETTUCCINE WITH CALAMARI AND SNOWPEAS

250 g young calamari (squid), cleaned and cut into rings

milk

350 g fresh tomato fettuccine or 280 g dried

40 g unsalted butter

dash cognac or brandy

10 small snow peas (mangetout), topped, tailed and halved

salt and white pepper

1 to 2 pinches pure saffron powder

¾ cup (180 ml) cream

AFRICAN HERITAGE GIFT SHOP AND GALLERY

1 Cover calamari rings with milk and soak for 45 minutes.

2 Cook fettuccine in boiling salted water.

3 Drain calamari, reserving milk, and fry quickly in melted butter until tender, 1 to 2 minutes. Add cognac and cook, stirring, until evaporated. Add 3 tablespoons of the soaking milk and reduce slightly before adding the snow peas. Season with salt and pepper and add saffron, then cook briefly before adding cream. Heat until slightly thickened.

4 When fettuccine is *al dente*, drain, then transfer to warm plates. Spoon sauce over pasta then serve. Let guests toss their own.

Serves 4 entrées

Tomato Fettucine with Calamari and Snowpeas (above) and Seafood Agnolotti with Coriander and Zucchini (below)

SAFFRON PASTA WITH SCALLOPS AND BLACK CAVIAR

PASTA

3 g pure saffron powder

2 teaspoons warm water

2½ cups (300 g) plain flour or 1¼ cups (150 g) plain flour and 1 cup (150 g) semolina

large pinch salt

3 eggs

SAUCE

350 g fresh scallops, soaked in milk to cover for 30 minutes

25 g butter

salt and white pepper

1 to 2 teaspoons Pernod or Ricard

1¼ cups (300 ml) cream

1 tablespoon black caviar or lump fish roe

1 TO PREPARE PASTA: Mix saffron in water and set aside for 10 minutes. Pile flours and salt onto a work surface and make a well in the centre. Add eggs with saffron and water to the centre and begin blending in the flours, using a fork. When you have a roughly amalgamated dough, use your hands and knead until a smooth, elastic dough is obtained, adding more flour or water as necessary. Shape into a ball, wrap in plastic or a damp cloth, and rest for 30 minutes. If preferred, the dough can be mixed in a food processor.

2 Divide the ball into four. Working one at a time, roll the balls out using a rolling pin or a hand-cranked pasta machine. When you have obtained long, even sheets of tagliatelle thickness cover again and rest for at least 10 minutes before proceeding. Now cut the pasta into tagliarini width, about 5 mm.

3 TO PREPARE SAUCE: Remove scallops from milk with a slotted spoon, reserving milk. Melt butter in a frying pan and fry scallops until just opaque. Season lightly, and add Pernod. Turn up the heat and cook, stirring, until most of the liquid has evaporated. Remove scallops and set aside. Add cream to the pan and boil until thickened.

4 Cook tagliarini in boiling salted water for 1½ to 2 minutes. Taste the sauce for salt and pepper, and then stir in scallops to heat through. When pasta is *al dente*, drain and quickly stir through a little vegetable oil before distributing between warmed plates. Spoon the sauce on top and then sprinkle with caviar; let the guests toss their own serving.

SERVES 4 AS AN ENTRÉE

FRESH HERB FETTUCCINE WITH SMOKED SALMON AND ASPARAGUS

PASTA

1⅔ cups (200 g) plain flour or 1¼ cups (150 g) flour and 1 cup (150 g) semolina

pinch salt

2 teaspoons finely chopped fresh parsley

2 teaspoons finely chopped fresh basil

2 eggs

SAUCE

350 g fresh asparagus spears, trimmed, peeled and halved

30 g butter

150 g sliced smoked salmon, cut into strips

1 cup (250 ml) cream

freshly ground black pepper

1 TO PREPARE PASTA: Pile flour and salt on a work surface and make a well in the middle. Add herbs and eggs and begin to incorporate into the flour, using a fork. When you have a loosely coherent dough, use your hands and knead it, adding a little flour or water if necessary for it to become smooth and elastic. Knead for at least 6 minutes and then rest, covered with plastic or a damp cloth, for 30 minutes.

2 Divide the dough into two and roll each half out into a thin, even sheet using a rolling pin or a hand-cranked pasta machine. Rest again, covered, for 10 minutes before cutting the sheets into fettuccine. Set aside but only cover if you feel the pasta will crack before cooking it.

3 TO PREPARE SAUCE: In a large saucepan of boiling water put the bottom halves of the asparagus; boil for a minute before adding the tops and continue to cook until tender. Remove with a slotted spoon and rinse under cold water. Drain, and when cool enough to handle cut each half into halves again, discarding any woody sections. Top up the pan of water and bring back to the boil. Begin cooking the fettuccine.

4 In a large frying pan melt butter and add smoked salmon. Sauté gently for 30 seconds before adding cream. Increase the heat a little and cook to thicken, then add black pepper generously and toss in asparagus.

5 When pasta is *al dente*, drain and transfer to the pan with sauce. Toss through, then serve with freshly grated Parmesan and the pepper mill handed around at the table.

SERVES 4 AS AN ENTRÉE

≈ FRESH HERB PASTA

Pasta flavoured with fresh herbs makes a wonderful base for light, fresh sauces. Herbs and vegetables which are in season at the same time, like the basil and asparagus in this recipe, often make perfect partners and require little else to flavour the dish. Along with the taste, the attractive appearance of green herbs through the pasta is reason enough to serve it with just melted butter and grated cheese. Try basil pasta with a cold sauce made from fresh ripe tomatoes, or fettuccine flavoured with fresh sage coated with a creamy Gorgonzola sauce.

SWORDFISH WITH ZUCCHINI AND SAFFRON

3 zucchini (courgettes), julienned

40 g unsalted butter

500 g fresh swordfish (or bonito or bluefin tuna) fillets, cut into 3 to 4 cm slices

2 small onions, thinly sliced

1 clove garlic, crushed

pinch pure saffron powder

½ teaspoon salt

½ teaspoon freshly ground black pepper

½ cup (125 ml) chicken stock

½ cup (125 ml) cream

500 g fresh fettuccine or 400 g dried

¼ teaspoon nutmeg

¼ teaspoon curry powder

1 Sprinkle zucchini with a little salt and let drain in a colander for 30 minutes.

2 Melt half the butter in a large pan and fry swordfish until just cooked through. Remove with a slotted spoon and set aside.

3 Add remaining butter to the pan and sauté onions and garlic until soft. Add saffron and seasonings and stir to coat. Add stock and cream and reduce over a medium heat.

4 Begin cooking the fettuccine in boiling salted water.

5 When the sauce is smooth and thick, add drained zucchini and poach for 1 minute. Add swordfish and heat through.

4 Drain pasta when it is *al dente*, transfer to a warm serving dish and pour the sauce over just before serving.

SERVES 4 AS AN ENTRÉE OR LIGHT MEAL

≈ SAFFRON

Saffron comes from the autumn crocus flower. It can be bought in two forms: powdered or strands. The strands have to be steeped in a little water to draw out their flavour and colour or can be lightly toasted to intensify the colour.

≈ **RIGATE**

This term is used to describe pasta which is ridged or grooved. It helps the sauce cling to the pasta.

SHELLS STUFFED WITH BACON, SPINACH AND RICOTTA

To serve shells as an hors d'oeuvre, bake them at 180°C (350°F) until the cheese is golden; this tends to give a firmer textured pasta which is easier to pick up with the fingers. Cook a couple more shells than is needed, just in case one or two tear during cooking.

12 giant pasta shells

1 teaspoon olive oil

1 clove garlic, crushed

100 g pancetta or bacon, cut into 1 cm pieces

4 canned Italian tomatoes

1 tablespoon fresh breadcrumbs

¼ cup (60 ml) cream

700 g ricotta cheese

250 g finely chopped, well-drained, cooked spinach

1 teaspoon chopped fresh basil or ½ teaspoon dried

2 tablespoons grated Parmesan cheese

good pinch nutmeg

salt and freshly ground black pepper

extra grated Parmesan cheese

1 Cook pasta shells, stirring once or twice, until tender but firm. Drain, rinse under cold water and drain again. Set aside.

2 Heat oil in a frying pan and sauté garlic and bacon until fat is extracted from the bacon and it becomes slightly crisp, 2 to 3 minutes.

3 Squeeze tomatoes with your hand over the sink, shake off excess juice and add pulp to the pan. Stir in breadcrumbs and fry briefly, then add cream. Cook for a further 1 to 2 minutes, stirring well, until the mixture is quite dry.

4 Place ricotta in a bowl with the bacon mixture, spinach, basil, Parmesan and nutmeg; mix well. Season with salt and pepper and a little more nutmeg if required.

5 Stuff each pasta shell with some of the filling and place them close together in a shallow heat-proof dish.

6 Sprinkle remaining filling and extra Parmesan over the top and place under a hot grill until the cheese is melted and golden.

SERVES 4 AS AN ENTRÉE

PASTA WITH ROASTED RED CAPSICUM

5 large, deep red capsicums (peppers)

350 g ridged pasta such as penne rigate, rotelli or conchiglie

2 tablespoons extra virgin olive oil

2 tablespoons olive oil

2 tablespoons finely chopped fresh basil or 3 tablespoons fresh parsley

3 anchovy fillets, drained and finely minced

2 cloves garlic, crushed

salt and freshly ground black pepper

1 Place capsicums under a hot grill and roast them until the skins are charred and blistered. Turn them to make sure that the entire surface is black. Remove and place in a large plastic bag while still hot. Tie off the bag well and leave for 30 minutes, when the charred capsicum skins can be removed easily. Remove seeds and slice capsicums into 5 cm lengths. Sprinkle with a little of the extra virgin olive oil and set aside.

2 Begin cooking pasta in boiling salted water.

3 Heat olive oil in a frying pan and sauté basil, anchovies and garlic for 1 minute on a low heat. Stir through capsicum and season with salt and pepper. Add extra virgin olive oil and cook over a low heat to develop the flavour.

4 When pasta is *al dente*, drain and toss through sauce with a couple of roughly torn basil or parsley leaves.

SERVES 4

Shells Stuffed with Bacon, Spinach and Ricotta (above) and Pasta with Roasted Red Capsicum

Cannelloni are not difficult to make, but they can be time-consuming. If fresh sheets of tomato pasta are unavailable, use plain pasta. This dish has a refreshing flavour which is ideal for serving in warmer weather, and as the dish can be prepared in advance, no slaving over a hot stove is necessary.

SALMON WITH LEMON CANNELLONI

TOMATO PASTA

2½ cups (300 g) plain flour

pinch salt

2 eggs

2 tablespoons double concentrate tomato paste (concentrated tomato purée)

FILLING

500 g ricotta cheese

880 g canned pink salmon, drained (reserve liquid)

juice 1 lemon

1 large egg, lightly beaten

2 tablespoons finely chopped onion

½ teaspoon salt

SAUCE

120 g butter

⅔ cup (70 g) plain flour

½ teaspoon salt

¼ teaspoon each white pepper and nutmeg

2¾ cups (700 ml) milk

reserved liquid from salmon

grated rind 1 lemon

GARNISH

1 tablespoon chopped fresh dill

1 TO PREPARE PASTA: Sift flour and salt onto a work surface and make a well in the centre. Lightly beat eggs with tomato paste and pour into flour well. Gradually work flour using a fork until a roughly combined dough is formed. Then begin kneading to obtain a smooth dough. It may be necessary to incorporate extra flour if the dough is moist to the touch. Shape into a ball, cover with plastic or an upturned bowl, and rest for 30 minutes.

2 Divide dough into two and roll each ball out into a thin, even sheet using a rolling pin or a hand-cranked pasta machine. Trim into rectangles 12 x 12 cm and over.

3 TO PREPARE FILLING: Place all ingredients in a bowl and combine well.

4 TO PREPARE SAUCE: Melt butter in a saucepan and stir in flour. Cook gently over low heat until smooth and slightly coloured. Stir in salt, pepper and nutmeg. Gradually pour in milk, stirring constantly, and cook until smooth and thick. Add reserved salmon liquid and lemon rind and set aside to cool.

5 Preheat oven to 180°C (350°F).

6 TO ASSEMBLE CANNELLONI: Cook the pasta sheets, a couple at a time, in boiling salted water until *al dente*. Remove with a large slotted spoon and layer on dry tea towels to drain. Trim edges to desired size. Put a thick line of filling along the length of each sheet and roll up to obtain filled tubes. Spread one-third of the sauce over the bottom of a shallow ovenproof dish, then place in the cannelloni tubes side by side. Pour remaining sauce over the top, covering all exposed pasta. Sprinkle with chopped dill and bake until bubbly, about 30 minutes.

SERVES 4 AS AN ENTRÉE OR LIGHT MEAL

GORGONZOLA AND WALNUT RAVIOLI

PASTA

3½ cups (435 g) plain flour

large pinch salt

4 eggs, beaten lightly

FILLING

250 g ricotta cheese

80 g Gorgonzola cheese

½ cup (60 g) walnuts, chopped

50 g Parmesan cheese, grated

2 tablespoons toasted fresh breadcrumbs

1 egg, beaten, to seal pasta

SAUCE

40 g butter

½ cup (125 ml) cream

grated Parmesan cheese

1 TO PREPARE PASTA: Sift flour and salt into a pile on a work surface, making a well in the middle. Add eggs and begin to incorporate the flour, using a fork. Continue until you have a loosely blended dough. Using your hands, knead the dough until a smooth and elastic ball forms, about 6 minutes. Cover with plastic or a damp cloth and let rest for 30 minutes.

2 Divide dough into four and, working one-quarter at a time, roll each out to a very thin, even sheet, using a rolling pin or a hand-cranked pasta machine. Rest the sheets of pasta, covered, while you make the filling.

3 TO PREPARE FILLING: Combine all ingredients except egg in a food processor or blender and mix until a coarse paste is obtained.

4 Working 1 sheet of pasta at a time, cut out 5 cm squares and put a little filling in the centre of each. Paint round the rims with beaten egg, then fold over diagonally to form triangles and press the cut edges together. Trim the cut edge with a zigzag pastry wheel or a crimper cutter, then put aside in a single layer until the rest are completed.

5 In a large pot of boiling salted and oiled water poach the ravioli, a few at a time, until done, about 4 minutes. Transfer to a warm serving dish.

6 TO PREPARE SAUCE: Melt butter, add cream and simmer until slightly thickened. Pour over ravioli, add 1 or 2 tablespoons of Parmesan, and toss lightly before serving. Serve with extra Parmesan and the black pepper mill passed around.

SERVES 4

PORK AND VEAL TERRINE

100 g ditalini or other very small pasta

1 small green capsicum (pepper), seeded and roughly chopped

150 g carrots, peeled and sliced

4 cloves garlic

2 onions, roughly chopped

2 tablespoons chopped fresh parsley

8 rashers bacon

1 heaped teaspoon dried thyme

1.5 kg pork and veal mince

¾ cup (45 g) fresh breadcrumbs

2 eggs, lightly beaten

1 teaspoon nutmeg

salt and freshly ground black pepper

1 Cook pasta in boiling salted water until *al dente*. Drain and rinse under cold water, then drain again.

2 Preheat oven to 180°C (350°F).

3 Put capsicum, carrot, garlic, onion and parsley into a food processor or blender and process until they are chopped finely, almost a purée. Transfer mixture into a large bowl.

4 Finely chop 2 bacon rashers by hand, and add them to the bowl with thyme, mince, breadcrumbs and eggs. Combine lightly, then add nutmeg, generous shakings of salt and pepper, and lastly the pasta. Mix well so that all the ingredients are evenly distributed.

5 Shape into a fat log and wrap with remaining bacon rashers loosely but evenly. Place in a shallow baking dish and bake for 1½ hours.

SERVES 6 TO 8

≈ **PORK AND VEAL TERRINE**

This loaf is as good cold as hot so it's an ideal choice for a picnic. It keeps well and slices beautifully as a tasty crust forms during baking.

Chicken Rolls with Paglia e Fieno

SPANISH STYLE FRESH TUNA AND LASAGNETTE

1 tablespoon olive oil

600 g fresh tuna, swordfish or other member of the tuna family

50 g prosciutto or unsmoked bacon, chopped

½ cup (125 ml) white wine

3 medium-sized onions, cut in quarters

2 cloves garlic, cut in half

350 g lasagnette, broken in half

1 tablespoon grated cooking chocolate

1 tablespoon dried breadcrumbs

1 cup (250 ml) veal stock

few celery leaves, to garnish

1 Put olive oil in the bottom of a flameproof pot, add tuna and top with bacon, wine, onions and garlic. Cook over a medium heat for 5 minutes, turn the tuna and cook for another 5 minutes. Lower heat and cook, covered, for 1½ to 2 hours.

2 Cook lasagnette in boiling salted water twenty minutes before serving.

3 Remove fish from the pot and keep warm. Add chocolate, breadcrumbs and stock, stir them through the remaining contents and bring to the boil. Simmer for 4 to 5 minutes, then strain through a fine sieve. If a thicker sauce is desired, transfer it to a smaller saucepan and reduce quickly.

4 When pasta is *al dente*, drain and transfer to a warm serving dish. Top with pieces of fish, pour over sauce and serve with celery leaves scattered on top.

SERVES 4

VILLA ITALIANA

CHICKEN ROLLS WITH PAGLIA E FIENO

4 chicken fillets

100 g prosciutto or raw smoked ham, finely chopped

50 g butter, softened

6 canned artichoke hearts, drained and quartered

salt and freshly ground black pepper

plain flour

2 tablespoons olive oil

1 small onion, finely chopped

½ cup (125 ml) dry white wine

⅔ cup (160 ml) chicken stock

400 g fresh spinach and plain fettuccine or 300 g dried

2 to 3 sprigs fresh bay or lemon leaves, to garnish

Parmesan cheese, to serve

1 Flatten each chicken fillet with a mallet, being careful not to tear the flesh. Mix prosciutto with half the butter and spread this mixture over the chicken slices. Top each with sections of artichoke heart, season, and then roll up around the stuffing and secure tightly with string or skewers. Season rolls lightly and coat with flour; set aside.

2 Heat remaining butter and olive oil in a flame-proof casserole dish and gently sauté onion for 5 minutes. Add chicken rolls and fry, turning, until brown on all sides. Add wine, season to taste and cook briefly to evaporate a little. Lower the heat and cook, covered, for about 30 minutes or until meat is tender. From time to time add some chicken stock to maintain an amount of gravy, and adjust seasoning if necessary.

3 Put fettuccine on to cook in boiling salted water. When *al dente*, drain and stir through a little olive oil. Transfer to a warm serving dish. Toss through gravy from the chicken.

4 Remove the skewers or string from the chicken rolls, arrange them on top of the pasta and decorate the dish with bay or lemon leaves. Serve immediately with freshly grated Parmesan.

SERVES 4

TAGLIATELLE WITH ASPARAGUS, HAM AND CREAM

500 g fresh asparagus

salt

400 fresh tagliatelle or 300 g dried

50 g butter

200 g prosciutto or unsmoked ham, cut into 3 cm strips

1 cup (250 ml) cream

freshly ground black pepper

2 tablespoons freshly grated Parmesan cheese

1 Put a large pan of water on to boil.

2 Peel asparagus, discard tough bottoms. Cut the tip of each spear off about 4 cm down, but keep the stalk in one piece.

3 Salt boiling water, add asparagus stalks, thickest ones first, and boil until half done. Add tips and continue boiling until tender but still crisp, stiff and bright green. Test as you go along. Remove from the water with a slotted spoon and cool slightly.

4 Into the boiling water put the pasta. Melt butter in a frying pan and add prosciutto. Fry until the butter begins to brown, but don't crisp the prosciutto. Add cream and bring back to the boil, lifting up the bits off the pan bottom while stirring. Add a few good grinds from the pepper mill.

5 Slice asparagus stalks into 4 cm lengths, discarding any tough bottoms. Add to the sauce with the tops and stir to coat; the cream should have reduced and thickened.

6 Drain pasta when it is *al dente* and turn into a warm serving bowl. Stir in the sauce and the Parmesan, toss to coat, and taste for salt and pepper before serving.

SERVES 4

≈ CHICKEN ROLLS WITH PAGLIA E FIENO

This dish looks splendid and is a great hit when served for a supper; the chicken rolls can be prepared earlier in the day to leave only the pasta for last-minute cooking.

≈ TAGLIATELLE WITH ASPARAGUS, HAM AND CREAM

Asparagus, Parmesan, butter and black pepper: there's no better combination of flavours and I can't think of any way to improve this dish, unless it were to beat an egg with the Parmesan and stir this through at the last minute.

Italian peeled tomatoes are recommended because they are deep red and ripe, sweet and full of flavour, and they are canned in thick natural purée which can be used elsewhere. However, it's a matter of shopping around and finding the brand you like.

BAKED TORTELLINI WITH EGGPLANT AND POTATO

250 g eggplant (aubergine), diced into 2 cm pieces

200 g tortellini, filled with beef or cheese

250 g potatoes, peeled and cut into 2 cm thick slices

½ cup (125 ml) olive oil

1 onion, thinly sliced

400 g canned Italian peeled tomatoes

½ teaspoon chopped fresh oregano or ¼ teaspoon dried

pinch cayenne pepper

salt and freshly ground black pepper

100 g fontina cheese, shredded

2 tablespoons extra chopped fresh oregano or parsley

1 Preheat oven to 150°C (375°F).

2 Sprinkle eggplant with salt and leave to drain over the sink in a colander or strainer.

3 Boil tortellini and when cooked drain and place in a shallow ovenproof dish.

4 In a small saucepan, boil potatoes until just cooked. Drain. Heat some oil in a frying pan and sauté potatoes until brown, then add to the tortellini.

5 With a little more oil, sauté onion gently for 5 minutes, then add drained eggplant. Continue cooking, (add more oil if necessary), until eggplant is tender and golden.

6 Lightly drain tomatoes and add to the pan, breaking them up with a wooden spoon while stirring in. Add oregano, cayenne, salt and pepper. Cook for a further 5 to 8 minutes, or until the tomatoes have reduced and there is little liquid left.

7 Add to the dish with the tortellini and toss through with one-third of the fontina. Season again with a few grinds of black pepper and salt. Distribute the remaining fontina over the top and sprinkle with the extra oregano or parsley.

8 Bake for 10 minutes so that the cheese melts through and bubbles on top.

SERVES 4

BUCATINI WITH TOMATOES AND SEAFOOD

20 g butter

1 tablespoon olive oil

1 onion, finely chopped

3 cloves garlic, crushed

1 teaspoon finely chopped fresh parsley

good pinch thyme

1.2 kg canned Italian peeled tomatoes, drained and puréed

salt and freshly ground black pepper

¾ cup (180 ml) fish stock or water

12 fresh or bottled baby clams, cleaned

150 g cleaned calamari (squid), sliced into rings

150 uncooked prawn meat (shrimp), cut into pieces

150 g white fish fillets, cut into pieces

½ to 2 teaspoons turmeric, to taste

1 g pure saffron powder (optional)

dash Pernod or Ricard (optional)

400 g bucatini

1 Melt butter and oil in a large pot and sauté onion and garlic over a low heat for 5 minutes. Add parsley and thyme, stir through then add tomatoes. Season with salt and pepper, raise heat slightly and cook covered, for 15 minutes.

2 Remove the lid and cook for a further 5 to 10 minutes, or until the sauce thickens. Add stock and bring to the boil. Add remaining ingredients and simmer until clams open and the seafood is cooked. Adjust seasoning. Discard any clams which have not opened.

3 Cook bucatini in boiling salted water. When *al dente*, drain and transfer to a heated serving dish, then toss through the sauce. (It is not usual to serve cheese with seafood sauces.)

SERVES 4

Baked Tortellini with Eggplant and Potato

≈ OLIVE OIL

*Pure olive oil is
chemically treated and
blended, but only with
other olive oils. It
contains no cholesterol.
Extra virgin olive oil is
generally made from the
first pressing of slightly
underripe olives, and
sometimes produced
without chemical means.*

BAKED EGGPLANT AND WHOLEMEAL FETTUCCINE

**400 g fresh wholemeal fettuccine
or 250 g dried**

2 eggplants (aubergines), cut into 1 cm slices

salt and freshly ground black pepper

⅓ cup (80 ml) olive oil

1 onion, chopped

1 clove garlic, crushed

**500 g fresh tomatoes, peeled, seeded
and chopped**

**2 teaspoons chopped fresh basil or
1 teaspoon dried**

4 zucchini (courgettes), sliced

250 g button mushrooms, sliced

2 tablespoons wheatgerm

2 tablespoons chopped fresh parsley

250 g mozzarella cheese, sliced

½ cup (125 ml) cream

1 Break fettuccine into thirds and cook in boiling salted water until *al dente*. Drain and set aside with a little olive oil stirred through to prevent sticking.

2 Lightly sprinkle eggplant slices with salt and stand to drain for 30 minutes.

3 Heat half the oil in a saucepan and gently sauté onion and garlic for 5 minutes. Add tomatoes, basil, salt and pepper and simmer, uncovered, until the sauce has thickened; about 12 minutes.

4 Preheat oven to 180°C (350°F).

5 Drain and dry eggplant. In a frying pan heat the remaining oil and sauté eggplant slices until golden; set aside. Fry zucchini, mushrooms and wheatgerm until tender, and then combine with the eggplant.

6 Arrange half the fettuccine in the bottom of a greased deep ovenproof dish. Sprinkle with half the parsley, then arrange half the eggplant mixture on this. Pour half the tomato sauce over the top. Repeat layering, then cover the last level of tomatoes with the mozzarella slices. Pour cream over the top and bake, uncovered, for 30 minutes.

SERVES 4 TO 6

TAGLIERINI WITH SARDINES

1 small fennel bulb

**12 fresh sardines, about 12 cm long, cleaned
and split open**

**½ cup (60 g) plain flour, seasoned with salt
and pepper**

½ cup (125 ml) olive oil

1 small onion, finely chopped

1 anchovy fillet, chopped

2 tablespoons toasted pine nuts

1 tablespoon sultanas

pinch pure saffron powder

freshly ground black pepper

**400 g fresh spinach and plain taglierini or
300 g dried**

1 Chop the green beards from the fennel and reserve. Trim the bulb, discarding any tough outer stalks, and finely slice enough to fill a quarter of a cup. Save the rest for another use.

2 Toss sardines in seasoned flour and fry them very gently in half the olive oil, a few at a time. Be careful when turning, not to break them up. Remove and keep warm.

3 Heat the rest of the oil and fry onion and fennel until soft. Add anchovy and fry, mashing as you stir, for 30 seconds. Add pine nuts, sultanas, saffron and a little black pepper. Stir and keep warm.

4 Cook taglierini in boiling salted water until *al dente*. Drain and put in a warm serving dish. Add the fennel sauce, toss through, and place sardines on top. Sprinkle with fennel greens and serve immediately.

SERVES 4

SPAGHETTI WITH CALAMARI

750 g fresh baby calamari (squid)

⅓ cup (80 ml) olive oil

1 large onion, finely chopped

3 cloves garlic, crushed

pinch chilli flakes

**600 g canned Italian peeled tomatoes,
drained and chopped**

salt and freshly ground black pepper

600 g fresh spaghetti or 450 g dried

2 tablespoons chopped fresh coriander

1 Remove head from squid and cut the tentacles straight across above the eyes. Discard head, keep tentacles and body, squeezing out the bony beak. If tentacles are a bit large, divide them into two. Remove the thin bone from the sacs and rinse them under cold water. Peel off the outer thin skin of each sac, washing under cold water as you go. If you feel the sacs are a little large, cut them into sections.

2 Heat oil and sauté onion, garlic and chilli gently for 5 to 6 minutes, until onion is soft and golden.

3 Add squid and cook until they turn opaque. Add tomatoes and season well with salt and pepper. Stir well, then lower the heat and cook, covered, for 30 minutes.

4 Cook spaghetti in boiling salted water until *al dente*. Drain and transfer to a warm serving bowl. Pour over sauce and toss through coriander just before serving.

SERVES 4

SPAGHETTI WITH CLAMS

1 kg small clams, washed and scrubbed

1 cup (250 ml) dry white wine

1 cup (250 ml) water

⅓ cup (80 ml) olive oil

2 cloves garlic, crushed

1 onion, finely chopped

800 g canned Italian peeled tomatoes, drained and chopped

2 tablespoons finely chopped fresh parsley

pinch chilli

40 g butter

salt and freshly ground black pepper

600 g fresh spaghetti or 400 g dried

1 Place clams in a large pan with wine, water and 1 tablespoon oil. Cover and cook over a high heat. As the clams open remove them with a slotted spoon; discard those

which don't open. Continue boiling liquid until roughly 1 cup (250 ml) remains; strain through muslin and set aside.

2 In a large pan heat remaining oil and sauté garlic and onion until golden. Add clam juice and let it evaporate a little before adding tomatoes, parsley, chilli and butter. Cook, uncovered, for 10 minutes over a medium heat. Season sauce and add a little more wine if it becomes too thick. Add clams and stir to heat.

3 Cook spaghetti in boiling salted water. When it is *al dente*, drain, and stir in a little olive oil to prevent sticking.

4 Transfer to warm bowls, top with sauce and serve with a small slice of butter on top of each dish, but no cheese.

SERVES 4

Spaghetti with Clams

≈ SPAGHETTI WITH CLAMS

Other shellfish can be included in the sauce, and the chilli can be left out if a less spicy dish is preferred. If only large clams are available, prepare them as below but remove the meat and discard most of the shells, saving just a few for decoration.

SHELLS AND SHELLFISH SALAD

400 g medium-sized conchiglie

1⅓ cups (330 ml) mayonnaise, preferably homemade

3 tablespoons chopped fresh tarragon or 2 tablespoons dried

1 tablespoon finely chopped fresh parsley

cayenne pepper

fresh lemon juice

1 kg cooked shellfish flesh: prawns (shrimps), lobster, crab, any one of these or a combination, cut into bite-sized pieces

2 mild red radishes, sliced

½ green capsicum (pepper), julienned

salt and freshly ground black pepper

Shells and Shellfish Salad

1 Cook pasta in boiling salted water until *al dente*. Drain, rinse under cold water and drain again. Place in a large bowl and stir through 1 to 2 tablespoons of mayonnaise.

Cool to room temperature, stirring occasionally to prevent sticking.

2 If using dried tarragon, simmer it in ¼ cup (60 ml) milk for 3 to 4 minutes; drain. Combine tarragon, parsley, cayenne, lemon juice and remaining mayonnaise and mix well.

3 Add shellfish to pasta with most of the radishes and capsicum, and salt and pepper. Mix through the tarragon mayonnaise and toss gently to coat. Cover, and chill before serving, adding more mayonnaise if the mixture is a little dry. Decorate with remaining radish and capsicum slices.

SERVES 8 AS A FIRST COURSE, 4 AS A MAIN MEAL

≈ PARSLEY

The parsley with the best flavour and leaf is the flat-leafed Italian or Continental variety. Dried parsley is simply not a good alternative in any recipe requiring fresh parsley.

VILLA ITALIANA

LASAGNE WITH PRAWNS AND ARTICHOKE HEARTS

800 g canned Italian peeled tomatoes, drained and pulped

1 clove garlic, crushed

salt and freshly ground black pepper

pinch chilli flakes

½ teaspoon finely chopped fresh basil or ¼ teaspoon dried

¼ cup (60 ml) olive oil

225 g dried lasagne sheets or 300 g fresh

350 g shelled cooked prawns (shrimps), halved if large

6 canned artichoke hearts, each cut into 6

2 tablespoons chopped fresh parsley

100 g mozzarella cheese, sliced

8 to 10 thin anchovy fillets

1 Preheat oven to 200°C (400°F).

2 Put tomatoes, garlic, salt, pepper, chilli flakes, basil and olive oil in a shallow ovenproof dish. Stir to combine and bake for 25 to 30 minutes.

3 While the tomato sauce is baking, cook lasagne sheets until *al dente*; drain, and place on dry tea towels in one layer.

4 **TO ASSEMBLE LASAGNE:** First grease a rectangular ovenproof dish. Put a thin layer of tomato sauce on the bottom and cover with a single layer of pasta. Combine the rest of the tomato sauce with prawns, artichoke hearts, parsley, salt and pepper. Now alternate layers of sauce and pasta, finishing with a layer of sauce. Cover this with slices of mozzarella and top with a lattice pattern of anchovies.

5 Lower heat to 180°C (350°F) and bake for 40 minutes, or until golden on top.

SERVES 4

ROAST BEEF WITH ROTELLI

½ cup (125 ml) olive oil

40 g butter

2 kg onions, thinly sliced

1 kg pot-roasting beef or brisket

100 g diced pancetta or bacon

1 stalk celery, chopped

1 carrot, chopped

sprig fresh marjoram or ½ teaspoon dried

salt and freshly ground black pepper

1 cup (250 ml) dry white wine

2 tablespoons water, beef stock or cream

500 g fresh rotelli or 350 g dried

1 Preheat oven to 150°C (300°F).

2 Melt 2 tablespoons oil and the butter in a large Dutch oven. Add onions and sauté over a low heat until golden and tender, at least 15 minutes. Transfer to a plate.

3 Heat remaining oil in the pot and brown the roast on all sides. Add pancetta or bacon and fry for a short time before adding celery and carrot, marjoram, salt and pepper. Fry these for 1 to 2 minutes and then return onions to the pot with half the wine. Mix in the vegetables well and cook for a minute until the raw wine aroma dissipates, then cover the pot and transfer to the oven.

4 Bake for 2 to 2½ hours or until the meat is tender. Add more wine as the juices reduce. A rich, dark gravy should surround the beef. Transfer the meat to a carving tray and keep warm.

5 Take off 1½ cups (375 ml) of the gravy and place in a blender or food processor with 2 tablespoons of water, beef stock or cream. Blend until you have a smooth thick sauce. Transfer to a small saucepan to keep hot.

6 Cook pasta in boiling salted water. Drain and serve with the onion sauce and grated Parmesan as the first course. Carve the beef and serve it with its gravy for the main course.

SERVES 5 TO 6

≈ **ROAST BEEF WITH ROTELLI**

The beef is also delicious served with a hot fresh tomato sauce instead of the gravy. Yellow and green button squash are an attractive vegetable to serve as an accompaniment; potatoes are not usually served with the main course.

*This chicken is excellent
served cold on a picnic.
The flesh remains moist
and succulent and the
stuffing becomes a side
salad. Those bacon
rashers which didn't
burn during the roasting
can be crumbled and used
in other dishes, e.g. tossed
through a green salad or
used as flavouring in a
pasta sauce.*

ROAST CHICKEN WITH PASTA STUFFING

150 g small shaped dried pasta (pennete or ditali)

12 spring onions, white parts only, thinly sliced

12 pistachio nuts, shelled

2 tablespoons finely chopped mixed fresh herbs (parsley, basil, sage or oregano)

5 canned Italian peeled tomatoes, drained and pulped

1 rasher bacon, cut into small pieces

¼ teaspoon salt

½ teaspoon freshly ground black pepper

50 g butter, softened

1 kg fresh chicken

1 slice bread

4 extra bacon rashers

1 Cook pasta until three-quarters done then drain it.

2 Preheat oven to 200°C (425°F).

3 In a large bowl combine spring onions, pistachio kernels, herbs, tomatoes, diced bacon, salt and pepper with the pasta.

4 Using half the butter, roughly grease the inside of the chicken, and fill it with the pasta stuffing. Place a slice of bread inside the opening to keep the stuffing in, fold flaps of skin over it and skewer tightly closed.

5 Rub the chicken over with the remaining butter and place it on its side on a rack in a baking dish. Sprinkle the body with a little ground black pepper and cover it with the extra bacon rashers. Roast for 20 minutes.

6 Turn the bird over onto its other side, sprinkle over a little more ground black pepper, cover with the bacon and put back into the oven for a further 20 minutes.

7 Now remove the bacon, turn the bird onto its back and roast again, basting often with the juices in the dish. After 20 minutes test to see if the chicken is cooked. If a skewer pushed into the thick flesh of a thigh produces liquid with a red tinge, roast the

bird for a further 5 minutes and test again. When the juices come clear it's time to take the chicken out. Rest it for a couple of minutes in a warm place before carving.

SERVES 2

FUSILLI AND SNAPPER BAKED IN A PARCEL

100 g fusilli

80 g butter

1 clove garlic

1 red capsicum (pepper), cut into strips

600 g snapper fillets or other white fleshed fish, cut into bite-sized pieces

100 g button mushrooms, sliced

2 teaspoons each chopped fresh parsley and fresh dill

salt and freshly ground black pepper

½ cup (125 ml) cream

2 tablespoons dry white wine

1 Cook fusilli in boiling salted water until not quite *al dente*. Drain and toss through a little vegetable oil to prevent sticking.

2 In a frying pan melt butter and gently sauté garlic clove and capsicum for 2 minutes. Add snapper fillets and sauté until just opaque. Add mushrooms, sauté briefly and then discard garlic. Stir in parsley and dill, season well and add cream. Cook until cream bubbles and then stir in the fusilli.

3 Preheat oven to 200°C (400°F).

4 Divide the mixture between four large sheets of aluminium foil or greased parchment. Season again lightly, sprinkle each with ½ tablepoon wine and fold up parcels, sealing well to prevent steam escaping. Place in a large shallow baking dish and bake for 20 minutes. Open carefully to let the steam out and serve immediately.

SERVES 4

SPAGHETTI WITH LAMB AND RED CAPSICUM

40 g butter

2 tablespoons olive oil

3 red capsicums (peppers), cut into thin strips 3 to 4 cm long

1 onion, finely chopped

3 cloves garlic, crushed

500 g lamb, cut into small dice

2 teaspoons vinegar

400 g canned Italian peeled tomatoes, drained and chopped

¼ teaspoon chilli flakes

salt

dry white wine

600 g fresh spaghetti or 450 g dried

40 g pecorino cheese

1 to 2 tablespoons finely chopped fresh parsley

1 In a heavy-based casserole dish heat half the butter and oil and gently sauté capsicums for 5 minutes. Remove from the pot with a slotted spoon and set aside.

2 Add remaining butter and oil to the pot and sauté onion, garlic and lamb over a medium heat until the lamb is lightly browned. Stir in vinegar, cover and leave for 10 minutes before proceeding.

3 Add tomatoes, chilli flakes and cooked capsicum, season with salt and cook the sauce for 5 minutes. Lower the heat and cook, covered, for a further 30 minutes, stirring once or twice. Add a little wine from time to time if the sauce begins to dry. Adjust seasoning if necessary.

4 Cook spaghetti in boiling salted water until *al dente*. Drain, and transfer to a warm serving dish. Pour over sauce and add pecorino and parsley. Toss together lightly and serve with more pecorino handed round at table.

SERVES 4 AS A MAIN COURSE

≈ **RED CAPSICUM (PEPPER)**

The darker the colour, the sweeter they are, and the more concentrated the flavour, especially if grilled or roasted.

≈ **PECORINO CHEESE**

This was originally made from sheep's milk. It is sharper and more piquant than Parmesan.

RIGATONI WITH SAUSAGE AND FRESH MARJORAM

20 g butter

1 tablespoon olive oil

1 onion, chopped

1 carrot, julienned

1 bay leaf

75 g bacon, chopped

200 g spicy Italian sausage, skinned and sliced

400 g canned Italian peeled tomatoes

salt and freshly ground black pepper

½ cup (125 ml) beef or chicken stock

400 g rigatoni

1 heaped tablespoon chopped fresh marjoram or oregano

1 Heat butter and oil in a frying pan and cook onion and carrot with bay leaf until onion is transparent.

2 Add bacon and sausages and cook, stirring often, until brown.

3 Squeeze half the tomatoes dry over the sink, pulp the flesh with your hand and add to the pan. Add the rest whole and break up loosely with the spoon while stirring. Season well with salt and pepper and simmer for 30 minutes over a low heat, gradually adding stock as sauce dries.

4 Cook rigatoni in boiling salted water until *al dente*. Drain and transfer to a warm serving dish. Add marjoram and sauce, and toss together lightly before serving.

SERVES 4

≈ RIGATONI WITH SAUSAGE AND FRESH MARJORAM

The success of this sauce depends upon the quality of the sausages, and on fresh marjoram being used. The flavour is rich and spicy, and the appearance should be fresh and bright.

ININI OF NEUTRAL BAY

Rigatoni with Sausage and Fresh Marjoram

BAKED SNAPPER AND PENNE WITH CITRUS SAUCE

200 g penne

½ cup (125 ml) vegetable oil

4 small to medium snapper steaks or other white-fleshed fish, trimmed

2 to 3 cloves garlic, crushed

1 tablespoon chopped fresh coriander, plus some sprigs for decoration

⅔ cup (160 ml) tomato purée or juice from canned Italian peeled tomatoes

3 tablespoons fresh citrus juice: lime, lemon, Seville orange, or a combination

chilli flakes

1 Cook penne in boiling salted water until barely *al dente*. Drain and stir through a little vegetable oil to prevent sticking. Transfer to an ovenproof dish.

2 In a pan heat some of the oil and brown snapper on both sides. Transfer to the dish and lay side by side on top of the penne, covering it completely.

3 Preheat oven to 220°C (425°F).

4 In the frying pan heat remaining oil and gently sauté garlic. Add chopped coriander, and then tomato purée and citrus juice. Cook, stirring, until the sauce boils and gives off a citrus aroma.

5 Sprinkle in chilli flakes to taste, then pour sauce over snapper. Pour in a little water, about 3 tablespoons, to make sure all the pasta is moistened. Cover loosely with foil and bake for 25 to 30 minutes, or until snapper is tender. Decorate with coriander sprigs and serve from the dish.

SERVES 4

MEAT ROLL STUFFED WITH SPINACH AND HAM

MEAT MIXTURE

1 kg lean minced beef

2 eggs, beaten

1 teaspoon thyme

½ teaspoon each salt, black pepper and crushed garlic

1 onion, finely chopped

2 tablespoons finely chopped fresh parsley

½ cup (60 g) dried breadcrumbs

½ cup (125 ml) Marsala

1 teaspoon tomato paste (concentrated tomato purée)

SPINACH MIXTURE

170 g well-drained, cooked spinach, finely chopped

60 g cooked stellini or other tiny interestingly shaped pasta

60 g Cheddar cheese, grated

25 g Parmesan cheese, grated

¼ teaspoon each salt, pepper and nutmeg

100 g ham, finely chopped

TOPPING

3 tablespoons fresh breadcrumbs mixed with 3 tablespoons grated Parmesan

1 TO PREPARE MEAT MIXTURE: Thoroughly combine ingredients in a bowl.

2 TO PREPARE SPINACH MIXTURE: Combine ingredients well in another bowl.

3 Preheat oven to 180°C (350°F).

4 To assemble the roll, on a large sheet of foil flatten meat mixture into a rectangle approximately 0.5 cm thick, 15 cm long and 9 cm wide. Spread spinach mixture evenly over the top. Roll up, Swiss roll fashion, starting at one of the shorter sides and using the foil to lift and roll.

5 Sprinkle over topping and wrap loaf tightly in foil. Place in a small deep-sided baking dish and bake for 1½ hours. Rest for 5 minutes, still in the foil, before serving.

SERVES 6 TO 8

≈ **MEAT ROLL STUFFED WITH SPINACH AND HAM**
When served hot this loaf hardly requires a sauce as it is moist and succulent. Cold, it slices well for picnics and makes delicious sandwiches.

≈ FONTINA CHEESE

A soft, delicate cheese from the Piedmont region in Italy. It is slightly nutty and has good melting qualities.

≈ PARMESAN CHEESE

Wherever possible use Parmigiano Reggiano, the best quality Parmesan. Parmesan cheese is low fat with a very high protein content.

ZUCCHINI AND SAUSAGE LASAGNE

½ cup (125 ml) olive oil

2 small carrots, finely chopped

1 onion, finely chopped

2 staiks celery, finely chopped

200 g spicy sausages

⅔ cup (180 ml) dry white wine

800 g canned Italian peeled tomatoes, drained and chopped

salt and freshly ground black pepper

800 g small zucchini (courgette), sliced

½ teaspoon chopped fresh oregano or ¼ teaspoon dried

400 g lasagne sheets

250 g fontina cheese, shredded

80 g Parmesan cheese, grated

1 Heat half the oil in a pan and add carrots, onion and celery. Fry gently until softened.

2 Remove casings from sausages and discard. Add meat to the pan and break up with a wooden spoon when stirring. Fry until brown, then pour in wine. Increase heat and cook until juices have reduced by half.

3 Add tomatoes, lower heat and simmer for 40 minutes, stirring from time to time. Season to taste.

4 In a separate pan, heat the remaining oil and fry zucchini with a little salt and oregano until tender and golden.

5 Cook lasagne according to instructions and drain on dry tea towels.

6 Preheat oven to 190°C (375°F) .

7 In a greased deep rectangular ovenproof dish place a layer of pasta. Add a thin layer of sauce then some zucchini slices. Sprinkle with some fontina and Parmesan cheese. Continue this layering until all ingredients are used up, finishing with fontina and Parmesan. Bake for 30 minutes

SERVES 6 TO 8 AS A MAIN MEAL

TAGLIATELLE WITH VEAL, WINE AND CREAM

Rich and filling, this dish makes an ideal meal served with a mixed salad. For a lighter sauce, the cream can be omitted and it's just as delicious.

500 g veal scallopine or escalopes, cut into strips

flour seasoned with salt and pepper

50 g butter

1 onion, sliced

½ cup (125 ml) dry white wine

3 to 4 tablespoons beef stock or chicken stock

⅔ cup (160 ml) cream

salt and freshly ground black pepper

600 g fresh tagliatelle or 400 g dried

freshly grated Parmesan cheese

1 Coat pieces of veal with seasoned flour and fry quickly in melted butter until browned. Remove with a slotted spoon and set aside.

2 Add onion to the pan and sauté gently until soft and golden, 8 to 10 minutes. Pour in wine and cook rapidly until the raw wine smell disappears, then add stock and cream and season with salt and pepper. Reduce again, and add veal towards the end.

3 Cook tagliatelle in boiling salted water until *al dente*. Drain and transfer to a warm serving dish.

4 Check the sauce for salt and pepper, stir in roughly 1 tablespoon Parmesan, pour it on the pasta and toss through. Serve with extra Parmesan handed round.

SERVES 4

Tagliatelle with Veal, Wine and Cream

ENDINGS

At the end of the day or the end of a meal, pasta works beautifully. With interesting textures and tastes of its own, it also provides the perfect foil for other flavours. In this section we have included recipes for luscious desserts, light suppers and delicious midnight snacks.

PASTA SOUFFLÉ

3 cups (750 ml) milk

grated rind ½ small lemon

2 teaspoons salt

250 g dried spaghetti or tagliatelle

80 g butter, softened

½ cup (125 g) sugar

3 large eggs, separated

½ cup (90 g) sultanas, soaked in
3 tablespoons brandy

¾ cup (90 g) chopped blanched almonds

pinch ground cinnamon

1 Preheat oven to 200°C (375°F).

2 Put milk, lemon rind and salt in a large saucepan and bring to the boil. Add pasta and gently cook, covered, until the pasta is tender, about 8 minutes. Remove the lid and set the pan in cold water to cool.

3 Cream butter and sugar together until smooth and light. Add egg yolks one at a time, beating well after each addition. Combine this mixture with milk and pasta, sultanas and brandy, almonds, and cinnamon.

4 Beat egg whites until stiff and loosely fold into the pasta mixture. Turn into a large buttered souffle dish and bake for 45 to 60 minutes. The top should be lightly browned and the centre set or, if preferred, slightly custardy.

SERVES 4 TO 6

NEUTRAL COUNTRY

This is a delicious dessert. Cook 300 g small conchiglie until just al dente. Drain and rinse in cold water. Stir a teaspoon of oil through and cool. Sprinkle a selection of fresh fruit (melon, kiwi fruit, peaches, mixed berries) with some fresh orange juice and lemon juice and a little sugar. Chill. Mix some yoghurt with honey, vanilla and Cointreau. Toss through pasta to coat. Pile pasta up on a large plate and surround with fruit. Decorate with toasted almonds and fresh mint leaves.

SWEET PASTA CAKE

250 g fresh spaghetti or 200 g dried

30 g butter

2 tablespoons caster sugar

⅓ cup (60 g) mixed peel

⅓ cup (60 g) sultanas

¼ cup (30 g) almonds

3 tablespoons dried figs or dates, chopped

2 tablespoons glacé cherries, chopped

2 tablespoons plain flour

½ teaspoon cinnamon

2 eggs, beaten

1 Cook pasta in boiling salted water until *al dente*. Drain, rinse under cold water and drain again. Transfer to a bowl.

2 Preheat oven to 180°C (350°F).

3 Melt butter in a small saucepan. Add sugar and heat, stirring, until sugar dissolves. Leave to cool.

4 In a large bowl, combine well mixed peel, sultanas, almonds, figs, glacé cherries, flour and cinnamon. Mix through pasta, then add butter-sugar mixture and eggs. Toss to coat.

5 Transfer mixture to a greased 20 cm ovenproof pie dish and level it out. Bake until set and golden on top, about 35 minutes. If the top browns, cover loosely with foil. When done, remove from oven and leave for 20 minutes before turning out.

Serves 6 to 8

CHESTNUT AGNOLOTTI

700 g moist fresh pasta sheets, thinly rolled

FILLING

450 g chestnut purée

2 tablespoons honey

2 tablespoons cocoa powder

2 tablespoons ground almonds

1 teaspoon cinnamon

1 teaspoon vanilla essence

2 teaspoons rum

3 tablespoons mixed peel, finely chopped

¾ cup (45 g) fresh breadcrumbs

1 tablespoon caster sugar

To Assemble

beaten egg for sealing

vegetable oil for frying

melted honey and icing sugar, to finish

1 To Prepare Filling: In a bowl blend all ingredients to form a smooth paste.

2 Working one sheet of pasta at a time and using a cookie cutter, cut out circles about 6 cm in diameter. Paint round the rims with beaten egg, then place some filling to one side of centre. Fold the pasta over to form a half-moon shape, and press the edges together. Run around the cut edge with a zigzag pastry wheel or a crimper cutter, and put to one side in single layers.

3 When all are made, heat some oil about 1 cm deep in a shallow frying pan until a slight haze is visible. Fry agnolotti, a few at a time, until golden on both sides. Remove with a slotted spoon and drain on absorbent paper. Serve warm with honey drizzled over the top and sprinkle with icing sugar.

Serves 4

SWEET RICOTTA AND FUSILLI

200 g fusilli

150 g ricotta cheese

pinch salt

3 teaspoons caster sugar

¼ teaspoon vanilla essence

¼ teaspoon grated lemon rind

¼ teaspoon cinnamon

heated milk

julienned lemon rind for decoration

1 Cook fusilli until *al dente*.

2 In a bowl, blend ricotta, pinch salt, sugar, vanilla, lemon rind and cinnamon. Add just enough hot milk to make a smooth sauce.

3 Drain fusilli and toss through ricotta sauce. Serve immediately, decorated with lemon rind and sprinkled with cinnamon.

Serves 4

PASTA WITH FRUIT AND NUTS

280 g rigatoni or other large, hollow tubes

100 g dried figs, softened in boiling water
15 minutes and finely chopped

½ cup (60 g) toasted blanched almonds,
finely chopped

½ cup (60 g) walnuts, finely chopped

¼ cup (30 g) raisins, chopped

2 tablespoons marmalade

grated rind 1 large orange

pinch ground cloves

¼ teaspoon cinnamon

100 g butter, melted and browned

caster sugar

vanilla ice cream, melted

1 Preheat oven to 190°C (375°F).

2 Cook rigatoni in boiling salted water
until just *al dente*. Drain, rinse under cold
water and drain again. Stir through a little
vegetable oil and set aside.

3 In a bowl combine figs, almonds, walnuts,
raisins, marmalade, orange rind and spices
and mix well. Stuff each pasta tube with
filling (use an icing bag with a large nozzle).
Place in a single layer in a greased, shallow
ovenproof dish. Pour over butter, sprinkle
with sugar and bake for 10 to 14 minutes.
Serve immediately with melted ice cream.

SERVES 4

ALMOND TORTE

4 cups (1 litre) milk

1 cup (220 g) sugar

1 cup (200 g) risoni

2 tablespoons vanilla essence

1 cup (120 g) blanched almonds

1½ tablespoons extra sugar

1 tablespoon dried breadcrumbs

6 eggs

3 tablespoons almond liqueur

1 teaspoon almond essence

1 In a large saucepan combine milk with
sugar, and bring to the boil. Add risoni and

Almond Torte

1 tablespoon vanilla essence and boil for
10 minutes, stirring once to twice. Set aside.

2 Preheat oven to 150°C (300°F).

3 Put almonds close together on a sheet of
foil on a baking tray. Sprinkle with the extra
sugar and some water and place under a hot
grill until caramelised. Chop coarsely with
breadcrumbs in a food processor or by hand.

4 Beat eggs, almond liqueur and essence,
and remaining vanilla essence together. Add
risoni mixture and almonds and mix well.
Pour into a greased shallow 25 cm dish and
bake for about 1 hour, or until the top is
golden brown and the torte set.

5 Remove from the oven and immediately
prick holes over the entire surface with a
toothpick or skewer. Sprinkle generously
with additional almond liqueur and let cool.

SERVES 6 TO 8

4 Preheat oven to 180°C (350°F).

5 Working one sheet at a time, place half teaspoons of jam at evenly spaced intervals along and across its length. Paint between the jam along the cutting lines with beaten egg. Cover this sheet with another one and run along the cutting lines with your finger to seal the two sides together. Cut out the ravioli with a floured zigzag pastry wheel. Repeat with the remaining sheets of pasta.

6 Brush the ravioli with beaten egg and place on a buttered baking tray. Bake until crisp and golden, about 30 minutes. Cool slightly and serve dusted with icing sugar.

SERVES 4

VILLA ITALIANA

Preparing Sweet Ravioli

SWEET RAVIOLI

1 cup (125 g) potato flour

1 cup (125 g) plain flour

pinch salt

½ cup (125 g) caster sugar

60 g butter

1 egg

grated rind 1 lemon

2 tablespoons milk

thick jam for filling

beaten egg for sealing

≈ SWEET RAVIOLI VARIATIONS

These ravioli can be served as a dessert with cream or mascarpone, or alone with coffee. They can also be deep-fried instead of baked, in which case they have a crisper pastry, but don't keep. If deep-frying, omit brushing the ravioli with beaten egg.

1 To make the pasta by hand, sift flours, salt and sugar together and then cut in the butter. Add remaining ingredients except jam and mix to form a dry but pliable dough, using a little more milk or extra flour if needed. Cover and rest for 1 hour.

2 If using a food processor, mix dry ingredients briefly (using the metal blade) and then add butter and egg. Mix for a couple of seconds before adding the rest of the ingredients and continue processing until the dough forms a ball and slows or stops the machine. Rest for 1 hour, covered.

3 Divide dough into quarters, then roll out each piece into a very thin sheet about 30 cm long. Cover with plastic or damp cloth.

SWEET CHEESE IN LEMON PASTA

These lemon parcels can be prepared earlier in the day and kept in the refrigerator, loosely covered, until ready to cook. Experiment with the size and shape of them; they look very good made smaller in a more traditional ravioli size.

PASTA

2 cups (250 g) plain flour

½ teaspoon salt

1 teaspoon caster sugar

grated rind 2 lemons

2 tablespoons fresh lemon juice

1 small egg, beaten

FILLING

600 g cottage cheese

⅔ cup (155 g) sugar

¾ cup (120 g) candied lemon peel

80 g dark chocolate, grated

½ teaspoon vanilla essence

1 tablespoon brandy

TO ASSEMBLE

beaten egg for sealing

vegetable oil for frying

1 cup (250 ml) cream, flavoured to taste with brandy

caster sugar

1 TO PREPARE PASTA: Pile flour, salt, sugar and lemon rind on a work surface and make a well in the centre. Add lemon juice and egg and begin blending them into the flour, using a fork. When a loosely combined dough is obtained, use your hands and knead it, incorporating extra flour as you go to form a smooth, dry elastic ball. Cover with a damp cloth or plastic and rest for 15 minutes.

2 Divide the ball into four and, working one-quarter at a time, roll each out to give a very thin sheet of pasta. Cover each sheet as it is completed. Rest again while you are preparing the filling.

3 TO PREPARE FILLING: Combine all ingredients thoroughly.

4 Cut pasta into 18 cm squares. Working a few at a time, brush round the edges of each pasta square with a little beaten egg. Place some filling in the middle of each and fold it in, like an envelope, to completely enclose. Press the edges down to seal tightly.

5 Pour some oil into a pan to 1 to 2 cm depth and heat it until a slight haze is given off. Fry parcels, one or two at a time, until golden on both sides. Remove with a slotted spoon and drain on absorbent paper; keep warm while the remainder are cooking. Serve warm with brandy cream and sprinkled with caster sugar.

SERVES 4 TO 6

*Sweet Cheese in
Lemon Pasta*

This dish is embarrassingly easy but is always a show stopper when served as the finale of a dinner party. The pasta can be prepared earlier in the day and kept moist, and the orange can be grated beforehand as well.

This is rich and delicate and so easy to make. Sauté 90 g pistachios in 125 g melted butter until golden. Add 40 g poppy seeds and 1 tablespoon sugar and stir to coat. Toss through 250 g farfalle, cooked.

CHOCOLATE FETTUCCINE WITH ORANGE BUTTER

CHOCOLATE PASTA

1 cup (150 g) semolina, durum wheat if possible

¾ cup (100 g) plain flour

1 tablespoon drinking chocolate powder

1 teaspoon cocoa powder

pinch salt

1 egg, lightly beaten

1 teaspoon vegetable oil

ORANGE BUTTER

150 g unsalted butter

1 large orange

1 TO PREPARE PASTA: Sift dry ingredients together. Gradually mix in egg and oil, adding a little water if necessary, to form a dry but well-combined dough. (Alternatively, dough can be mixed in a food processor.) Now knead it on a lightly floured board for 6 to 7 minutes to give a smooth and elastic ball. Rest for at least 15 minutes.

2 Divide dough in two and roll each half out into a thin rectangular sheet roughly 20 cm long. Let the pasta sit for a few minutes before cutting. Either cut the sheets into fettuccine using a hand-cranked pasta machine, or roll each up along its length and slice off the ribbons with a sharp knife.

3 Cook the pasta in boiling salted water.

4 TO PREPARE ORANGE BUTTER: Peel rind off one-quarter of the orange, remove any pith left on the rind and slice it very thinly into 2 to 3 cm lengths. With a very fine grater, grate the zest off the rest of the orange, being careful not to collect any of the pith.

5 In a small saucepan heat butter until it browns slightly. If the butter fats begin to separate, strain the butter into another saucepan and proceed. Add orange rind and zest. Heat gently for 2 to 3 minutes until orange rind gives off its distinctive aroma.

6 Drain cooked pasta and quickly pour the sauce over it. Serve immediately with lightly whipped cream or mascarpone.

SERVES 4

CHOCOLATE NUT CAKE

250 g farfalle

1 cup (170 g) roasted hazelnuts

1½ cups (150 g) walnut halves

¾ cup (100 g) blanched almonds

2 tablespoons dried breadcrumbs

3 tablespoons cocoa powder

40 g dark chocolate, grated

1 teaspoon cinnamon

⅔ cup (155 g) sugar

1 tablespoon mixed peel, finely chopped

grated rind 1 lemon

1 teaspoon vanilla essence

3 tablespoons cognac

1 Cook pasta in boiling salted water to which has been added a teaspoon of sugar. When it is barely done, drain.

2 Chop nuts and breadcrumbs together in a food processor until a coarse paste forms. Transfer to a bowl and mix with the rest of the ingredients. Stir about ½ cup of this mixture through the warm pasta.

3 In a greased deep-sided round casserole spread a thin layer of nut paste. Cover this with a layer of pasta, then another of the paste, continuing until fillings are used up. Finish with a topping of nut paste. Cover cake with a flat plate just big enough to fit into the dish, and press down well. Store in a cool spot or refrigerate for at least 12 hours, pressing on the plate from time to time.

4 Serve at room temperature and decorate with some extra grated chocolate or a dusting of icing sugar. Cut the cake into wedges while still in the dish. Serve with coffee or as a dessert with whipped cream.

MAKES 12 TO 16 SLICES

MEASURING MADE EASY

HOW TO MEASURE DRY INGREDIENTS

15 g	½ oz	
30 g	1 oz	
60 g	2 oz	
90 g	3 oz	
125 g	4 oz	(¼ lb)
155 g	5 oz	
185 g	6 oz	
220 g	7 oz	
250 g	8 oz	(½ lb)
280 g	9 oz	
315 g	10 oz	
345 g	11 oz	
375 g	12 oz	(¾ lb)
410 g	13 oz	
440 g	14 oz	
470 g	15 oz	
500 g	16 oz	(1 lb)
750 g	24 oz	(1½ lb)
1 kg	32 oz	(2 lb)

QUICK CONVERSIONS

5 mm	¼ inch	
1 cm	½ inch	
2 cm	¾ inch	
2.5 cm	1 inch	
5 cm	2 inches	
6 cm	2½ inches	
8 cm	3 inches	
10 cm	4 inches	
12 cm	5 inches	
15 cm	6 inches	
18 cm	7 inches	
20 cm	8 inches	
23 cm	9 inches	
25 cm	10 inches	
28 cm	11 inches	
30 cm	12 inches	(1 foot)
46 cm	18 inches	
50 cm	20 inches	
61 cm	24 inches	(2 feet)
77 cm	30 inches	

NOTE: We developed the recipes in this book in Australia where the table-spoon measure is 20 ml. In many other countries the tablespoon is 15 ml. For most recipes this difference will not be noticeable.

However, for recipes using baking powder, gelatine, bicarbonate of soda, small amounts of flour and corn-flour, we suggest you add an extra teaspoon for each tablespoon specified.

Many people find it very convenient to use cup measurements. You can buy special measuring cups or measure water in an ordinary household cup to check it holds 250 ml (8 fl oz). This can then be used for both liquid and dry cup measurements.

MEASURING LIQUIDS

METRIC CUPS

¼ cup	60 ml	2 fluid ounces
⅓ cup	80 ml	2½ fluid ounces
½ cup	125 ml	4 fluid ounces
¾ cup	180 ml	6 fluid ounces
1 cup	250 ml	8 fluid ounces

METRIC SPOONS

¼ teaspoon	1.25 ml
½ teaspoon	2.5 ml
1 teaspoon	5 ml
1 tablespoon	20 ml

OVEN TEMPERATURES

TEMPERATURES	CELSIUS (°C)	FAHRENHEIT (°F)	GAS MARK
Very Slow	120	250	½
Slow	150	300	2
Moderate	160-180	325-350	3-4
Moderately hot	190-200	375-400	5-6
Hot	220-230	425-450	7-8
Very hot	250-260	475-500	9-10

Published by Murdoch Books®,
a division of Murdoch Magazines Pty Limited,
213 Miller Street, North Sydney NSW 2060.

Photography: Ashley Barber
Styling: Michelle Gorry
Front cover photograph by Rowan Fotheringham, with styling by Donna Hay. (Spicy Ricotta Agnolotti in Herb Leaf Pasta; plate from Costa de Fiori, Darlinghurst.)

Murdoch Books® Associate Food Editors: Kerrie Ray, Tracy Rutherford. Publisher: Anne Wilson. Publishing Manager: Catie Ziller. Production Coordinator: Liz Fitzgerald. Managing Editor: Susan Tomnay. Creative Director: Marylouise Brammer. International Manager: Mark Newman. Marketing Manager: Mark Smith. National Sales Manager: Karon McGrath. Photo Librarian: Dianne Bedford.

National Library of Australia Cataloguing-in-Publication Data:
Glynn, Joanne. The new pasta cookbook. Rev. ed. Includes index.
ISBN 0 86411 517 2. 1. Cookery (Pasta). I. Title. (Series: Bay Books cookery collection). 641.822. First published in Australia in 1988. This edition 1996. Printed by Griffin Press, Adelaide.

INDEX